Towards Freedom

TOWARDS FREEDOM

Critical Essays on Rabindranath Tagore's *Ghare Baire/The Home and The World*

Edited By
SASWATI SENGUPTA.
SHAMPA ROY,
SHARMILA PURKAYASTHA

Orient BlackSwan

TOWARDS FREEDOM

ORIENT BLACKSWAN PRIVATE LIMITED

Registered Office
3-6-752 Himayatnagar, Hyderabad 500 029 (Telangana), INDIA
e-mail: centraloffice@orientblackswan.com

Other Offices
Bangalore, Bhopal, Bhubaneshwar, Chennai, Ernakulam, Guwahati, Hyderabad, Jaipur, Kolkata, Lucknow, Mumbai, New Delhi, Noida, Patna

First published 2007
Reprinted 2015

ISBN: 978 81 250 3187 1

Typeset in 11/14 pt. Adobe Garamond

Typeset by
Bukprint
Delhi

Printed in India at
Glorious Printers
Delhi

Published by
Orient Blackswan Private Limited
1/24 Asaf Ali Road
New Delhi 110 002
e-mail: delhi@orientblackswan.com

In memory of
Professor Sisir Kumar Das (1936–2003)

বড় কঠিন সাধনা যাঁর বড় সহজ সুর

To such an arduous vocation, so simply was he attuned

Contents

WORLD/*BAIRE*

Acknowledgements

This anthology was conceived and conceptualised during the fortnightly seminars held by the English Department of Miranda House. The encouragement and support of all our colleagues in the department have been immense. While teaching this text to first-year English Honours students, the need was felt for a student friendly anthology on the subject. The result is this volume. It acknowledges the enthusiasm of the students to the teaching of *Ghare Baire* in class.

The sudden demise of Professor Sisir Kumar Das on 7 May 2003 was a blow, as he was to be one of the main contributors. His words of encouragement and his belief in the project inspired us to carry it forward in his absence.

We wish to thank the contributors who readily agreed to write for this anthology. Given that the contributors are recognised scholars and experts in their fields, the alacrity with which they responded to the project has been very encouraging. We are grateful to Gothe for his technical expertise and interventions and also to the team at Orient Longman.

Our final acknowledgement is to Debjani M. Dutta, publisher and friend. Her immediate positive response coupled with warm friendly sessions on the book and other matters has been very helpful and enjoyable.

Notes on Contributors

SEKHAR BANDYOPADHYAY teaches Modern Indian History at Victoria University of Wellington, New Zealand. He is the author of numerous articles and books and his most recent ones are, *From Plassey to Partition and After: A History of Modern India* and *Caste, Culture and Hegemony: Social Dominance in Colonial Bengal.*

SUMANTA BANERJEE is based in Dehra Dun and is engaged in research on popular culture and social history of nineteenth-century Kolkata. He is the author of several works including *Parlour and the Street: Elite and Popular Culture of Nineteenth Century Calcutta, Under the Raj: The Prostitute in Colonial Bengal,* and *Logic in a Popular Form: Essays on Popular Religion in Bengal.*

SAMBUDDHA CHAKRABARTI is a practising lawyer and is based in Kolkata. He received his PhD from Calcutta University and is the author of *Andare Antare: Unish Satake Bangali Bhadramahila*, a seminal book on the status of women in Bengali society in the nineteenth century.

SHIRSHENDU CHAKRABARTI is Professor of English at the Department of English, Delhi University. He has published extensively on modern Bengali literature and has translated Tagore's writings into English and also translated certain English texts into Bengali. He is also a poet and has published a volume of poetry in Bengali in 2001.

SHARMILA PURKAYASTHA teaches English in Miranda House. She has co-authored "Prison House of Orientalism" with Zakia Pathak and Saswati Sengupta. The article critiques Edward Said's work, *Orientalism,* from the perspective of the Indian classroom.

NIHARRANJAN RAY (1903–1981) was Professor of Fine Arts and Ancient History and Culture at the University of Calcutta. He wrote extensively on a vast range of subjects, and his most well known is the magnum opus of Bengali history titled, *Bangalir Itihaash.* He has received several prestigious awards such as the Sahitya Akademi Award and the Padmabhushan.

SHAMPA ROY teaches English in Miranda House and has done her PhD on the "Representation of Indian Women in British Colonial Texts". Her work involves the study of British women writers writing on India in the colonial period.

SASWATI SENGUPTA teaches English in Miranda House and has done her PhD on the *Brata Kathas* of Bengal, Orissa, and Assam. She has also co-authored the articles "Prison House of Orientalism" (1993) and "Between Academy and the Street: A Story of Resisting Women" (1997). Both have been extensively anthologised.

1

Introduction

Rabindranath Tagore's *Ghare Baire* was first serialised in 1915 and published as a novel in 1916. The English translation, with some excisions, by Surendranath Tagore was published in 1919 as *The Home and The World*.[1] The events narrated in the novel belong to the period 1905–08, a period of tremendous political unrest in Bengal in the wake of the partition of the province by the colonial British government and the rise of militant nationalism, historicised as *bangabhanga* and the swadeshi movement. This brief pre-Gandhian anti-colonial movement occupies an important place in the national historiography and even more so in the popular memory of middle-class Bengal despite its short duration and failure.

The partition of Bengal was effected on 16 October 1905 during the vice-royalty of Lord Curzon on the grounds that the premier province of the Bengal Presidency had grown too vast for effective administration. The administrative failure in dealing with the Orissa famine of 1866, for instance, was blamed on the vastness of the presidency and used to strengthen the argument for its partitioning.[2] The new province was to be called Eastern Bengal and Assam with its capital at Dhaka. However, the proposed partition of the province for the furnished reasons of greater administrative efficiency was perceived by the nationalists as "... little more than smokescreens for a deep Imperialist design of 'divide and rule'."[3] The educated middle-class Bengalis saw in this proposal a deliberate move to splinter the solidarity of the Bengali-speaking population and their growing nationalism along communal lines, as the partition would encourage the growth of a Muslim power in eastern Bengal. In his speech at Dhaka on February 1904, for instance, Lord Curzon had reminded the Muslims of "their superior culture" and promised that the British would "invest the Mohammedans in Eastern Bengal with a unity which they have not enjoyed since the days of the old Mussalman Viceroys and kings".[4] The political protest against the partition of Bengal that started in 1905 with a call to boycott British piece goods was known as the swadeshi movement.

The swadeshi protest among the upper-class Bengali circles over the territorial division was, however, not without material considerations. The partition of the province, which would lead to a Court of Appeal at Dhaka, the rise of local newspapers, the imminent prominence of the Chittagong port, was apprehended as loss of business for the Calcutta lawyers, journalists, and *zamindar*s who owned vast tracts of land across west and east Bengal. The growing unemployment within the educated *bhadralok* section, which coveted jobs in the Indian Civil Service, fuelled popular anti-British sentiments. All of these accounted for the high-caste Hindu bhadralok orientation of the swadeshi movement. The student community of Bengal also responded with great enthusiasm to the call of nationalism. Students, including schoolboys, participated *en masse* in the campaigns of swadeshi and boycott. The government retaliated with the notorious Carlyle Circular that aimed to crush the students' participation in the swadeshi and boycott movements, and the "Anti-Circular Society", a militant student organisation, came into being to oppose the repressive methods.[5]

Initially the swadeshi movement used "moderate" methods of press campaigns, meetings, and petitions. The failure of such techniques led to a more extreme demand. As Aurobindo Ghosh asserted, "We recognize no political object of worship except the divinity in our Motherland, no present object of political endeavour except liberty, and no method or action as politically good or evil except as it truly helps or hinders our progress towards national emancipation."[6] The new demand led to a search for new forms of agitation ranging from the aggressive boycott of British goods to terrorist activities. Rabindranath Tagore subscribed to the school that advocated the need for constructive self-help through swadeshi industries and National Schools which he termed "*atma shakti*" or self-strengthening. But between 1905–07, there was greater exhortation for a more relentless recourse to armed struggle. The Bengal extremists even got in touch with the Tilak group in Maharashtra and sought to give the Congress programme a new orientation at the Calcutta Congress of 1906.[7] Gradually, the swadeshi mood in general was closely linked with individual acts of heroic self-sacrifice and terrorism and attempts to colour the boycott movement with Hindu religious revivalism. The Hindu revivalist trend together with the British propaganda that the new province would mean more jobs for the Muslims splintered the appeal for communal unity, which drew from Tagore the admission that "Satan cannot enter till he finds a flaw...".[8] Rabindranath Tagore gradually withdrew from the political arena of the aggressive middle- and upper-class swadeshi movement.

The Hindu-Muslim riots between 1906–07 exposed the inadequacy of the movement to counter this communal challenge. Coercion soon brought resistance, and the constructive programmes of swadeshi were not enough to generate enthusiasm among Muslim and low-caste Hindu peasantry, resulting in the failure of the movement.[9] The two communities, outcaste and despised by the high-caste Hindu gentry, initiated their own counter-mobilisation campaigns in opposition to the swadeshi movement emanating from different historical consciousnesses and dissimilar ideological construction of the nation. The colonial government, at the same time, began to offer concessions, one such being that its employees in Eastern

Bengal and Assam would be recruited on the basis of proportional numerical strength of various communities. By 1908, the swadeshi movement was on the decline. The failure of the movement is related to the ideological limitations of the Hindu bhadralok, who drew sustenance from the liberal professions, intermediate tenures, and subordinate administrative services, and its inability to address labour unrest, offer a constructive economic plan to the peasants, dissolve sharpening communal tensions, or carry on consistent constructive work in the villages.

This public political upheaval takes place alongside another revolution—that of women's emancipation and a new gender equation in Bengal. The history of nineteenth-century Bengal is now widely recognised as crucial to the new construction of gender relations. The influence of Western education and philosophy on the traditional society of Bengal starts manifesting itself from the second and third decade of the nineteenth century. In a comparative evaluation of Western and Bengali social systems, the social position of women was marked as chief evidence of the latter's backwardness. Of all the debates and agitation about the social reforms of the nineteenth century, the majority of them centred on those that dealt with women's utter helplessness and position in society—*sati*, child marriage, incongruous age difference between bride and groom, condition of widows, polygamy, the need and extent of female education. In the nineteenth century, the question of equal right to education for men and women was not raised, but towards the close of the century, the belief that women should not be educated at all was on the decline. Journals and periodicals published in the second half of the nineteenth century foregrounded the need for improvement in the condition of women in the *antahpur*. Issues of female education, emancipation, as well as femine domestic virtues highlighted the progressive sections' attempt at gender reforms, and, at the same time, the patriarchal limits of colonised Bengali society.[10]

Ghare Baire is the first fictional exploration of the entangled web of crucial issues related to two spheres—The Home and The World—as implicated in questions of women's freedom and the nationalist project in early twentieth-century Bengal. Nikhilesh is an enlightened, introspective, upper-caste young zamindar who attempts to "emancipate" his wife. The wife, Bimala, strong and sensuous, is drawn in the process towards Nikhilesh's charismatic, swadeshi friend, Sandip. Sandip's brand of nationalism is communal, but holds the promise of power and the possibility of gender emancipation. The interposing, interior monologues of these three protagonists constitute the fictional rendering of the charged historical period. The contemporary response to the novel was dominated by the horrified condemnation of Bimala's modernisation. Her adulterous desire was berated for being shamelessly disruptive of traditional values, indicating the discomfiture of even the progressive sections of society with a novel that seemed to question so blatantly the mystified notions of chastity and domestic subservience of the Hindu wife. Surprisingly, the other important aspect of the novel—its critique of extremist nationalism through the figure of the morally dubious Sandip—did not receive much contemporary critical attention. As far as Western critical reception was concerned, besides the damning criticism of the novel that came from Lukacs, who characterised it as "a petit-bourgeois yarn of the silliest kind", most other critics passed it over, probably for not giving that message of "Eastern mysticism" with which they principally associated Tagore. His novels, in fact, remained largely ignored, dealing as they did with specific problems of contemporary Bengal and hardly fulfilling the requirements of "imagining India" in terms of spiritual transcendence, squalor, and chaos that had been standardised by writers like Forster and Kipling.

Subsequently, in the post-independence context, as Tagore went on to become a towering figure in the tradition of Bengali/Indian literature, critical response to the political questions and ideological debates in the text was governed by an admiration for Tagore's universal humanism and an easy identification of the author's politics with that of Nikhilesh's idealism. It was only later, with a rigorous historical analysis of the swadeshi movement, the politics of nation formation, and particularly in the interest of marginal/subaltern interests, and India's (and the world's) preoccupation perforce with fundamentalism and militant insurgencies that the political questions of motivations, methods, and the margins of "freedom" movements in the world and the text—were foregrounded.

What makes *Ghare Baire* relevant to our times? Turning to its context, precisely a hundred years after the 1905 partition of Bengal, one is struck by the rich ideological terrain ranging from gender reforms and education to caste mobilisation and nationalism; issues that hold relevance even today. The swadeshi context of the novel allows for questioning the politics of nationalism premised on caste hierarchy and religious intolerance, precisely because we see in the novel the possible birth of such a nation. The novel shows glimpses of the poor ryots' poverty-stricken life in the wake of swadeshi. Panchu's story is an extremely moving one as it shows how the feudal zamindars like Harish Kundu exploit and ruthlessly dominate poor tenants in the name of swadeshi. Distant echoes of the Permanent Settlement, the zamindar-peasant relationship, and the Hindu-Muslim conflict in rural Bengal reverberate through Tagore's narrative. But *Ghare Baire* is not essentially about class conflicts or contradictions. In fact, class configurations are presented sketchily and details are kept to a minimum except in the case of Nikhilesh and his household. And, while the text documents how Panchu is exploited by the swadeshi agitation, it offers little by way of analysis of why educated and yet unemployed students would be swayed by the ideology of anti-colonialism. Historically, the swadeshi agitation did not throw up two classes, the exploited and the exploiters, along with some benevolent intellectuals. The *andolan,* if anything, showed class alliances between zamindars and educated, unemployed young men, on the one hand, while the poor and exploited peasantry, both Hindus and Muslims, remained outside the andolan. Clearly, the representation of Nikhilesh as a rich zamindar who is anti-swadeshi is an intriguing aspect which raises questions of the nature of upper-class/caste feudal benevolence. Could there be a more complex trajectory of the low castes' struggle for identities during the period other than the patronising plot that Nikhilesh's (and Tagore's) narrative maps?

Militant nationalism in the novel centres on the issue of boycott of foreign goods, as does communalism. The active targeting of the Muslim peasantry together with hate speeches is a reminder of the majoritarian view built into the notion of nationhood. It is possible to "read" Tagore's uncompromising rejection of the communal agenda in Hindu nationalism, as represented by Sandip, in the light of communal carnages in recent history. But the fractured nature of communal issues in the novel—the fact that Muslims are represented as both rioters and marauders and, at the same time, victims of the swadeshi plot—makes sense only if one remembers that the representation of communalism is tied with other factors such as caste and class. Thus, the novel inserts instances of exploitation of the poor peasantry comprising both Hindus and Muslims who are, regardless of their religion, exploited by the zamindars and their agents. Swadeshi, however hardens religious identities on both sides.

True, reading is a moment in history, but to "only connect" Tagore's times with ours is not enough. There is the need to historicise, and understand the formations within which *Ghare Baire* is emplotted and drawn to troubled conclusions, for without that "connection"—recognition of similarities—it might mean an acceptance of history as an inevitable replication. *Ghare Baire* is not simply a quasi or reductive historical text. It is imaginative literature artfully written about the troubled swadeshi era well after the passion and urgency of the movement were spent. Artfully, because it uses sophisticated narrative methods like interior monologues, perspectivism, implied audiences, and fictional autobiographies. The shifting nature of the narrative frames a rich, ideologically charged story of politics, passion, and patriotism. Its politic play of history is its beginning, its conclusion, its plot, its characters, and the circumscribing of the tale's field of possibilities. The tale, the teller, the technique, the context—all hold out different and exciting possibilities of critical inquiry. The issues of caste, class, religion, gender, nation raised in the novel demand to be addressed.

And thus grew *Towards Freedom*, a collection of critical essays, out of a collective attempt to make meaning of the critical issues posed by *Ghare Baire* that became part of the B.A. English Honours syllabus in Delhi University a few years ago, when the old syllabus, which consisted largely of Western canonical writings, was overhauled and several non-Western, especially Indian writings, became part of the new curriculum. While postcolonial theorists would laud this curricular move for being one that frees students from the expectation to relate predominantly to the culture of "a vague space called Britain" and to submit to the "gradual cultural alienation" fostered by the "burden of English studies", does the inclusion of Indian texts alone signify "freedom"? It is of course important to recognise that one of the ways of challenging the orthodoxies of mainstream English studies is to open up the canon to non-Western writings. However, it is equally important to recognise that the rubrics of postcolonial criticism that make colonialism the "determining marker of history" or essentialise non-Western texts in terms of indigenous authenticity are highly restrictive if not suspect. The crucial and intermeshed issues of religion, region, class, caste, gender, etc., that are constantly demanding to be addressed within the Indian context (where we live and teach) get necessarily overlooked by the fetishisation of such rubrics. For us at the Miranda House English Department, where there has been a long tradition of enabling pedagogy that addresses the world outside the classroom, the importance of *Ghare Baire* lies in its being a complexly crafted novel that allows an engagement with issues of caste, class, and gender politics, relevant to both its moment of production as well as its reception. It cannot therefore simply be reduced to being an essentialised voice of indigenous authenticity striking back at the Empire.

Towards Freedom begins by tracing the history of the novel form in Bengal, often taken to be a by-product of colonial education, its relationship with the middle-class readership, and the relation between the form, the language, and the story. One of the aims of this anthology is to visibilise how imaginative literature constructs histories by examining the play of ideologies in this novel. Much of these structured hierarchies of oppression function powerfully in our lives outside the classroom, even today. The division of the book into two sections, 'Home' and 'World' is not, of course, meant in any way to signal the mutually exclusive or intrinsically separate nature of these two categories. It could hardly be otherwise given that the novel itself examines a critical moment in history when the boundaries between the domestic and the public become irretrievably blurred with the surging in of swadeshi ideas right into the sequestered interiors of the antahpur and the forcing of its sheltered inhabitant to confront much larger questions than those related simply to conjugality or domesticity. The contextual social history of Bengali bourgeois wifehood and domesticity frames the presentation of Bimala as the newly reformed wife, educated by both the husband and an English woman tutor, and who is simultaneously drawn to Sandip's project of gendering the nation. The private monologues of each of the three principal characters also bear testimony to their individual longings, frustrations, and self-searching as being inseparably linked to questions related to the larger political and social sphere and their historical location in such a world. Taking its cue then from the novel, the chapters of this book repeatedly examine the various ways in which the domestic space and the private relationships it shelters are in fact deeply crisscrossed by social and political relations. The structural division of *Towards Freedom* is thus for a heuristic and not a hortatory purpose.

Notes

1. *Ghare Baire* remains the primary text for the contributors of this anthology. Individual articles, however, indicate the text in Bengali or Surendranath Tagore's English translation.
2. "...He(Sir Stafford Northcote) referred to the famine of 1866 as furnishing evidence of the existing system of Government when exposed to the ordeal of a serious emergency, and among other methods of relieving the over-tasked administration, he suggested the separation from Bengal proper of Assam and possibly of Orissa." Letter by H.H. Risley, Secretary to the Govt. of India, in Nityapriya Ghosh and Ashoke Kumar Mukhopadhyay, eds., *Partition of Bengal: Significant Signposts 1905–1911,* Kolkata, Sahitya Samsad, 2005.
3. Sumit Sarkar, *The Swadeshi Movement in Bengal 1903–1908,* New Delhi, People's Publishing House, 1977, 12.
4. Ghosh and Mukhopadhyay, 25.
5. Ghosh and Mukhopadhyay, 95–96.
6. Sarkar, 65.
7. See Sekhar Bandyopadhyay, *From Plassey to Partition: A History of Modern India,* New Delhi, Orient Longman, 2004, 258.
8. Rabindranath Tagore, "Byadhi O Pratikar", (1907) *Rabindra Racanabali* XII, Kolkata, Sri Saraswati Press Ltd., 1962, 909.

9. For the swadeshi movement, see, Nityapriya Ghosh and Ashoke Kumar Mukhopadhyay, eds, *Partition of Bengal : Significant Signposts 1905–1911,* Kolkata, Sahitya Samsad, 2005. Also Haridas Mukherjee and Uma Mukherjee, eds, *Bande Mataram and Indian Nationalism 1906–08,* Calcutta, Firma KLM, 1957; Bipan Chandra, *The Rise and Growth of Economic Nationalism in India : Economic Policies of Indian National Leadership 1880–1905,* New Delhi, People's Publishing House, 1966. Bimanbehari Majumdar, *Militant Nationalism in India 1897–1917 and its Socio-Religious Background,* Calcutta, General Printers and Publishers Private Ltd., 1966. Sumit Sarkar, *Swadeshi Movement in Bengal, 1903–1908,* New Delhi, People's Publishing House, 1973; David L. Johnson, *The Religious Roots of Indian Nationalism. Aurobindo's Early Political Thought,* Calcutta, Firma KLM, 1973; Sekhar Bandyopadhyay, *Caste, Protest and Identity in Colonial India : The Namasudras of Bengal 1872–1947,* Curzon, Surrey, 1977; Rajat Kanta Ray, *Social Conflict and Political Unrest in Bengal 1875–1927,* Delhi, OUP, 1984.
10. For gender reform in colonial Bengal see, Ghulam Murshid, *Reluctant Debutante: Response of Bengali Women to Modernization, 1849–1905,* Rajshahi, Rajshahi Univ. Press, 1983; Partha Chatterji, 'The Nationalist Resolution of the Women's Question' in Kumkum Sangari and Sudesh Vaid, eds., *Recasting Women: Essays in Colonial History,* New Delhi, Kali for Women,1989, 233–53; Geraldine Forbes, *Women in Modern India,* Cambridge University Press, 1996; Tanika Sarkar, *Words to Win The Making of Amar Jiban: A Modern Autobiography,* New Delhi, Kali, 1999; Tanika Sarkar, *Hindu Wife, Hindu Nation,* New Delhi, Permanent Black, 2001.

2

The Role of Tagore's Literature

NIHARRANJAN RAY

If Rabindranath was the creator of the first effective short stories of Bangla literature, then Bankim was the one to have introduced to this literature its first significant novels[1]. It was Bankim who started combining the descriptions of starkly lit realities and conflict-torn lives within the flow of the social with complex analysis. This has remained till date the staple of our novels. But Bankim's work, for all its realism, was deeply inflected with the fantastic elements of romances. Though firmly rooted in reality, his novels are followers of the tradition of romances in their imaginative use of fantasy and the supernatural, flamboyant prose, and strident idealism within the rich tapestry of history. From the mid- to the late nineteenth century, this was largely the nature of novels in both European and Bangla literature. They were born of social necessity and out of their social contexts. It was with this legacy that Tagore began his journey of novel writing. But Tagore was not Bankim. His sensibilities were very different from that of his predecessor. Besides, the contexts of the two writers were different and their social consciousness was not the same.

The nature of these differences may be briefly studied for it might help to understand the nature of Tagore's novels. Bankim's consciousness was formed within the times and context that saw the first cultural expression of Western-educated and Western-influenced Indian consciousness. The intellectual upheaval that had taken place amongst the educated Bengalis in the first few decades of the nineteenth century, as a consequence of their conflictual relations/friction with the West, had begun to settle down by the later decades of the century. Educated Bengalis managed to recover their equipoise to a large extent, and rejuvenated and enriched by their new-found knowledge and ideas, they began to look at their own homes and community from new perspectives. Their own nation and its all-too-familiar surroundings seemed to acquire a certain novelty to them. Bankim was the first graduate from Calcutta University and, subsequently, under the new legislation, became the very first modern, educated Deputy Magistrate. In short, he represented the enlightened and educated middle-class Bengal of the times and of its social consciousness. This social consciousness was extremely complex.

The inevitable consequences of the Permanent Settlement established by Lord Cornwallis had begun to be gradually felt from the second quarter of the nineteenth century itself. Most of the old feudal families and royal dynasties, big and small, had died out as a result of the East India Company regime and in their place had sprung up a new class of exclusively landowning zamindars as well as a gradually expanding middle class of salaried men and professionals. Bankim belonged to this emergent educated middle class. At the time that he was writing, the lives and practices of this class, its particular joys and sorrows, conflicts and problems, had yet to assume a clear and specific shape. And, as far as the countless common folk were concerned, their existence was so miserable, so abject and downtrodden that they found no place in Bankim's consciousness, indeed none in the parameters of the consciousness of the contemporary educated middle class itself. Bankim found no interesting material for his writings in their lives, and it is quite possible that he made no conscious effort in that direction either. What remained then was the recently declined feudal society and the new class of landowning zamindars that drew its inspiration from the ideas, attitudes, and practices of the earlier aristocracy. It is these two social classes that then became Bankim's source material for his novels, and it was with the consciousness of a middle-class writer that he responded to their lives and practices.

As mentioned earlier, even though the old feudal aristocracy had practically died out, its memories still burned bright. The tales of its valour and chivalry, fiercely felt emotions and conflicting ideals, its independent spirit and glorious pride in belonging to ancient clans had just begun to arouse the imagination of the newly formed Western-educated middle class and to fill it with visions of the future. It is within this past, shadowy and unclear as it was, that the Westernised Bengali consciousness searched for some signs of the future and for a sense of national pride. Historical knowledge of this past was, however, as yet incomplete, fragmented, distorted, and vague. But, it was around this vaguely understood past that the romantic imagination of the contemporary writers took form. It was the same with Bankim. The end of the medieval period was the period of decline of Muslim rule. It was the period of administrative chaos and emptiness, and most of Bankim's historical novels were based in this period.Wherever historical knowledge was incomplete and fragmented, Bankim used his imagination to fill the gaps. But despite this, the partly known and at times completely unknown past was bound to remain shadowy, and it was precisely because of this that in a novel it needed the magical strokes and vibrant colours of romance and fantasy.

The powerful idealism discernible in Bankim's writings reflects the social consciousness of the educated middle class of his times. This idealism had been formed partly through the study of Mill, Bentham, Comte, and of the French Revolution and had partly drawn strength from the recent attempts to study India's past. The clash of these two kinds of ideologies gave rise to a new form of idealism within the minds of the educated middle class. A strong sense of nationalism and cultural identity were by far the most important components of this idealism. But it was also deeply inflected with religious and communal pride.

Bankim's creative imagination was also inspired by the new landowning aristocracy, and there is evidence of this in at least two of his novels. However, since Bankim was familiar with the consciousness of this class and since their lives did not belong to some obscure moment in the distant past but were part of the prevalent context, his novels based on them are largely realistic and the presence of the fantastic in them is quite restrained.

Like most educated individuals of his time, Bankim was a rationalist. As a result he felt compelled to search for causal connections between events and to analyse the psychology of characters. Such analysis is without doubt quite profound at times, but it never becomes adequately or uniformly probing such that the subtler aspects of character and plot development remain unexplored. For the most part such analytical powers reveal themselves suddenly in order to shed light on some particularly unusual incident or state of mind and then immediately afterwards recede from sight. In all probability, Bankim was not entirely conscious of these limitations, for his romantic imagination seems to have been much stronger than his realism.

Bankim died in the year 1894; Tagore was thirty-two years old at that time. His first novel, *Bouthakuranir Hat,* had been published in 1882 and his second novel, *Rajarshi,* in 1886. But his first significant novel *Chokher Bali* was written after ten years, in 1902, and it is in the novels written in this period that one begins to get a sense of Tagore's response to the social consciousness of his time. In fact, this response is much more clearly visible in his novels and short stories than in his poetry and songs. Even in the short stories, which are very lyrical, the social response remains somewhat attenuated.

In any case, the social changes that had taken place in Bengal between Bankim's period and that of Tagore's need to be looked at closely. By the end of the nineteenth century and the early decades of the twentieth, the class of Western-educated Bengalis was well established, and its nature had become clearly perceptible. Its thoughts and ideals, daily struggles and internal conflicts had taken a distinct shape in the last fifty years. This middle class was largely progressive, was in the forefront of most of the things happening in society, and it headed most of its institutions. The middle class in Bankim's time had not enjoyed this status. Besides, the status of the landed aristocracy was still intact at the time, and since the power and pride of this class had depended on social and legal systems related to landownership remaining unchanged, it was a class that was, in its attitudes and aspirations, conservative and opposed to progressive changes. Most members of this class had also kept themselves at a distance from Western education and thought. Only a handful came in contact with such ideas and developed a consciousness that seemed to be influenced and inspired in ways similar to that of the contemporary middle classes. The traces of this ancient feudal aristocracy were all but wiped out in the next fifty years. The memories of this class, which had earlier inspired and enthused the enlightened middle classes, no longer had that power in Tagore's time. These then in short were the differences between the time of Bankim and Tagore.

Tagore was the grandson of Prince Dwarakanath Tagore and the son of Maharshi Debendranath Tagore. The Tagore family of Jorashanko was exceptionally renowned for its gentility and refinement in contemporary upper-class society, and it had also become the site for the union of Hindu and Muslim cultural influences. Tagore's uniqueness lay in the fact that despite having been born and nurtured in this upper-class family and society, his mind principally drew its nourishment from the thoughts and ideas of the middle classes. His friends and associates like Priyanath Sen, Lokendranath Palit, Satishchandra Sen, Mohitchandra Sen, Ajit Chandra Chakrabarti, and many others were all from this class. It was the particular joys and sorrows of this class, the subtle and crude conflicts of its inner and outer worlds, its bitterness and excitement, hopes and aspirations, sadness and despair, its sense of personal freedom and cultural identity, that then became the source material for Tagore's stories and novels.

As described above, it was as a consequence of the differences in their social contexts that the novels of Tagore and Bankim were so different. With the fading away of the memories of the old feudal aristocracy, the historical novel too began to fade away. Bankim had managed to harmoniously combine historical memory with the experienced reality of the present social life and had created powerful historical novels. However, once that memory began to grow dim, the gaps and inadequacies in the historical knowledge of that past became very apparent. The vividly experienced realities of daily existence washed away those extravagant memories, and in their place what remained were the starkly felt conflicts and struggles of everyday lives, their pathos, frustration, and despair. Almost immediately, the romantic imagination and perspective associated with Bankim as well as the use of the supernatural and the fantastic became obsolete. Bankim's romance depended heavily on sudden and unexpected magical events of diverse kinds. These lost their validity in the creative expression of the social consciousness of the contemporary middle classes. Tagore was also a romantic, but his strain of romantic thought and perspective was quite different. Tagore's romanticism was based on the profound communion between human consciousness and nature, the transcendental mysteries of life, and the fine, deeply buried feelings of the heart. This romanticism was completely inward-looking, and it borrowed nothing from the vicissitudes of external events or the suddenness of supernatural occurrences. It was this romanticism that made the stories written by Tagore in his initial phase so deeply lyrical, and it was this that gave to his novels their poetic resonance and beauty.

As I have mentioned before, Bankim's social novels were to a large extent realistic, but the kind of nuanced and extensive analysis of causal connections that realistic writing necessarily depends on is missing in his novels. I have also briefly discussed why this was so. Where after all was the place for it within the profusion of colourful events and myriad characters of the historical novels? And even in the social novels, the analysis of life's experiences was so deeply coloured by the hues of the imagination and so brightly illumined by the light of glorified ideals that it always fell short of becoming a truly probing analysis. The middle-class lives that, on the other hand, became the source material for Tagore's novels were neither very eventful nor colourful. The natural flow of these lives was slow, even sluggish, and ordinary events occurred in them owing to very ordinary reasons. The conflicts, clashes, frustrations, guilt, and opposition that became visible in these lives followed from the conflicting elements embedded within the society. The picture that emerges in Tagore's novels is painted with immensely subtle and efficacious strokes. The day-to-day sorrows and joys, problems and conflicts are described with such fullness and with such a probing of the causes that the reader is strongly rooted in the sense of the real and is awakened to a keen awareness of diverse social attitudes and ideologies, in short, to an awareness of social life. In the short stories written in the later period as well as in his novels starting with *Chokher Bali*, it is this commitment to the real that has led to a prising open of the conflicts and contradictions that lie submerged within middle-class society. It is his awareness of these social contradictions that constitute Tagore's social consciousness. And it is this commitment to the real that distinguishes Tagore's novels from Bankim's writings. This realism that is manifested in Tagore's novels subsequently, alongside the changes within middle-class society, assumed new forms for disseminating the truth and a sense of reality.

Keeping then in mind the social background and the few things said in the preceding lines about Tagore's novels, we may now proceed towards a systematic critique of individual novels which have been taken up in the order of their publication.

Chokher Bali (1902)

If, within any literature, a single novel has ever managed to completely transform the prevalent form and nature of novel writing and has ushered in a whole new age of writing novels, then it has to be Tagore's *Chokher Bali.* Tagore wrote this novel after a gap of ten years. He had had several kinds of experiences in those years, and having developed a fine awareness of material realities, he was able to arrive at a better understanding of the social life around him. *Chokher Bali* is the first novel in Bangla literature based on social life and contains an analysis of psychological states and problems. Before this, novels in Bangla were mainly focussed on incidents. The clever plotting of such incidents was the principal feature of these novels. Tagore's own earlier works, *Bouthakuranir Hat* and *Rajarshi* had also followed this pattern. *Chokher Bali* was just the opposite of this. Those parts of the novel that carry the plot forward are brief; instead there are long sections devoted to the analysis of the psychological states of the four main characters. The description of incidents merely help in a better understanding of the development of these mental states. The entire story can in fact be narrated in a few lines; but that would only amount to a bare outlining of the plot without any sense of the narrative's realism. This sense of the real can be actually derived only by seeking to understand the diverse thoughts and emotions fleeting through the deepest recesses of the consciousness of Mahendra, Binodini, Behari, and Asha. It is only through this that one understands the significance of their external actions. This kind of analysis of the submerged causal relations between human thought and actions and of material realities made *Chokher Bali* the first novel of its kind.

It would perhaps not be irrelevant to discuss here how social realities are expressed in *Chokher Bali.* From the beginning of the twentieth century, new complexities of the social life in Bengal with its different ideologies and attitudes had become part of Tagore's literary concerns. The effects of the breakdown of the joint family system and of the old sense of community had begun to be felt even earlier. In fact, it is not difficult to see traces of these even in Bankim's novels. However, this sense became much stronger by the early decades of the twentieth century. The notions of individual freedom were becoming quite strong and the need to define the relations between the individual and society was felt urgently. This was of course still limited to a handful of educated middle-class men; for, as I have said earlier, it was this class which was the spokesperson for social progress. The problems of this class, its vision of the future, which was tied up with its sense of tradition, became the special features of Tagore's creative consciousness. The rebellion of individual identity and personal freedom against the demands and duties of joint family household and those of the larger community is expressed quite clearly in several places in *Chokher Bali.* This sense of personal freedom was not prepared to accept the "crushing out of the sweetly ripening juices of the newly wed young wife through incessant domestic work." Mahendra protests against this a number of times in the novel. The intensely private relations of husband and wife that a modern couple desire cannot grow in a natural and free manner within the joint family. Becoming the daughter-in-law of a large joint family ought not to be the only mark of a woman's identity. The other significant sign of her identity lies in the free and mutual relationship that she shares with her husband, which is separate from her roles within the joint family. It is this sense of freedom that has in modern Bengali society led women to think of and desire for identities in terms of womanhood alone, separate even from this shared conjugality. In Tagore's own later fiction one can see the emergence of this consciousness within the upper middle classes.

The need for sexual freedom is also a necessary expression of this sense of personal freedom. Even Bankim's creative consciousness did not remain impervious to the complex problems that rise out of this awareness. The character of Rohini in *Krishnakanter Will* bears witness to this. But since this awareness had yet to emerge very powerfully at that time and was for Bankim something entirely new and contrary to contemporary social thought, Rohini does not win Bankim's approval or even his sympathy. In Tagore's time, Rohini is transformed into Binodini. And even though the idea of a woman's assertion of freedom hurt prevalent cultural sensibilities, she does manage to create a place for herself within the readers' consciousness. The changed literary expression reflects the social changes from Bankim's time to Tagore's.

Gora (1908)

Gora was written in 1908 and was immediately serialised in the monthly magazine *Prabaashi*. *Gora* is the only novel in Bangla literature in which the social thought of the educated Bengali middle class, its aspirations and frustrations, its anxious search for new religious and community ideals, its intensely heated arguments, passions and excitement, intelligence and courage—in short its very life has been given form. In fact, in this novel, one sees a meaningful literary effort being made to explore in a larger sense the links between contemporary society and ideals of nationhood and the private relations between men and women. Truth to tell, it would be difficult to find a Bangla novel to date that could match the breadth of its context and the depth of its study of cultural identity. The characters of this novel are not represented in terms of their private lives alone; beyond such lives they are seen as having larger identities that are closely entwined with their social and cultural existence. Within its contemporary context, it is this that gives the novel its special character. In order to grasp the significance of this particular characteristic, a brief survey of the contemporary times in Bengal, the conflicts in its ideals related to religion, society, and nation, and Tagore's responses to these is required. From the end of the nineteenth century, a great deal of nationalist anger was gradually gathering force. The arrogance and injustices of the colonial government had begun to enrage the English-educated middle-class Bengalis. It was this nationalist rage that then became the source of a growing sense of a nationalist identity as well as of cultural soul-searching. From the end of the nineteenth century, many Indian scholars and thinkers from various regimes began to be engaged in the search for essential unities within the heterogeneous ideals of life and conflicting religious thought and cultures in India. This effort became even more pronounced in the early years of the twentieth century. Amongst these scholars in Bengal who became involved in such efforts, Tagore was the most significant. Tagore found the ideal of such unity within the self-renunciation, meditation, spiritual austerities and asceticism of ancient India and within the deeper meanings of the ideals of *varnashram*. This is indicated quite clearly in *Naivedya*. From 1902, as soon as he took on editorial responsibility of the new version of the *Bangadarshan*, he devoted himself to the propagation of these ideals. In the controversy that he became involved in with Ramendrasundar Trivedi over the question of social ills and their solutions, it was Tagore who first stated that it is not possible to think of a social malaise in a narrow sense. The malaise has to be located within the entire cultural life and it was from such a perspective that he then proceeded to analyse the nation's ideals and problems.

In his discussion of Western and Eastern ideals (*Bangadarshan* 1902) also, he has examined such ideals from different angles. His consciousness about the nation and nationalism, Hindus and Hindutva was also formed at about this time. It was also about this time that he became acquainted with Brahmobandhav Upadhyay. From such controversies, discussions, and acquaintances, there started emerging in Tagore's consciousness a strong and comprehensive philosophy and idealism regarding our culture, religion, society, and nation. This comprehensive philosophy is also indicated quite clearly in such lectures, essays, and critical pieces as *Brahman*, *Chinamaner Cheethi*, *Bangla Bhasha o Sahitya*, *Bharatbarsher Itihaash*, *Atyukti*, *Rashtraneeti o Dharmaneeti*, *Dharma Prachaar*. In the last mentioned lecture, he even states that when man begins to accept the pursuit of a particular kind of religion as his spiritual quest, then his religious quest actually becomes fragmented and impeded. For true religion is not confined to a particular time, place, rituals, sacred texts, and holy words. In these essays, discussions, and lectures there are arguments, reflections, and even a certain style of speech and expression that are then brought to life in the behaviour, conversations, and debates of the characters of *Gora*.

From the beginning of the andolan in 1904, the unbearable agony that had been accumulating for over a whole century began to be reflected in the thoughts and actions of the contemporary educated men and women. The andolan struck at the roots of the social and political thought of the educated middle classes. Tagore also did not remain cut off from all this. In fact, not only did he not remain cut off, he became one of its prime movers. There was the need to think anew about the nation and nationalism, but Tagore refused to put nationalism above the needs of the nation, and he sought to express the passion of the andolan in actual reformist activities. This is quite clearly expressed in his essay titled, *Swadeshi Samaj*. However, Tagore had also begun to notice that contemporary social and nation-related thought and ideals were becoming increasingly divisive and fragmenting. The narrow-mindedness of the leaders (of the andolan) and their working also became apparent to him. Often there would also be conflicts between the party workers. Young minds drawing their inspiration from

Sandhya, *Jugaantar*, and *Bande Mataram* were filled with terrorist and revolutionary ideas. Besides, the Hindu-Muslim riots of Jamalpur had also exposed internal fissures with an ugly starkness. Given the parameters of such thought and incidents, the transformation that took place within Tagore's social and nation-related reflections becomes evident for the first time in his essay titled, *Byadhi o Protikaar* (*Prabaashi* July 1908). Meanwhile, differences between sections of the Congress had reached their peak. The extremist revolutionary had turned to violent bombing tactics. In essays like *Poth o Pathheya*, *Samasya* , *Sadupaay*, and especially in the one called *Poorbo o Poshchim*, the changes in Tagore's social consciousness become clearly evident; the manner in which the Tagore of the swadeshi era was gradually transformed into a very different Tagore is quite clearly indicated in these writings and lectures. *Gora* is quite intimately linked to both these Tagores. The various characters of this novel have grown out of these specific thought processes and reflections. They cannot be understood fully if studied in isolation from their contemporary ideas and activities.

As mentioned earlier, the various characters of *Gora* have a social identity besides having a private life, and each of these individuals are acutely conscious of this larger identity; in fact so conscious are they that each one of them tries to establish it in terms of his or her specific beliefs and regulate their lives according to them. Each seems to be the spokesperson for a particular ideology. The web of their arguments and ideological conflicts occupy most of the novel. Pareshbabu's pure but impractical religiosity and belief in a life of truth, the tender-hearted Binoy's conflict-torn language, and Gora's own language through which the passionate excess of the Indian sense of self is forcefully expressed—all of these become so evident that as soon as we see these characters or even Panubabu, Anondomoyee, and the others we can predict which way their arguments and beliefs will flow and what turns they are likely to take. As a result, it has sometimes been alleged that the characters of *Gora* do not glow with sufficient brightness and lack depth.

The realism of this novel is in fact closely linked to its social consciousness. The effort to dismantle Gora's class and caste status is also related to this consciousness. The conflicts between traditional customs and conventions and the sexual independence of men and women as revealed through the events leading up to the marriages of Gora and Sucharita, and of Binoy and Lalita also indicate contemporary concerns. That all these characters are able to emerge successfully out of these conflicts reveal the progressive nature of Tagore's consciousness. Also by revealing the illusory and false nature of the philosophy that Gora had constructed by conflating the nation's culture with a rigid following of certain rituals, Tagore has indicated his progressive thinking. The urge to ground his activities on a firm pragmatic basis is quite clearly evident in Gora's endeavour. The fact that he walks along the Grand Trunk Road in a bid to familiarise himself with his country and to meet, understand, and love the people of the villages in order to have an easy relationship with them indicates, on the one hand, a romantic form of patriotic love and service and, on the other, an effort made by the writer to alert him to the realities of his country.

At the time that *Gora* was being written in Bengal, the Brahmo Samaj was engaged in intense controversies and arguments within itself and with the larger Hindu community over the question of religious and social ideals as well as of religious customs and rituals in ways that shook the entire educated middle class. Within the Brahmo Samaj, the question of Brahmo versus the larger meaning of Hindu had also led to conflicts and disagreements, and Tagore himself had participated keenly in these debates. *Gora* echoes all of this.

Ghare Baire (1916)

The novel *Ghare Baire* was serialised in *Sabuj Patra*. At the same times Tagore was writing poems for *Balaka* and several other prose pieces. The novel provoked controversies not just when it was completed, but even when it was being serialised on a monthly basis. Tagore himself also participated in these debates. A great deal of what came up in these controversies is irrelevant to a literary analysis of the novel. But, they provided Tagore with the occasion to articulate a few things about the relations between literature and society which are worth quoting over here. Once in a response to a query about novel writing, he had said that writers are like deer, which are commonly believed to be able to wonderfully camouflage their bodies but remain blissfully unaware of this ability. However, he goes on, "The times within which a writer is born probably reflects some of its ideas through the writer's work...For the context works within the writer at a conscious as well as at an unconscious level...The secret ways in which the modern period of our nation has left its mark on the writer's mind have been reflected in *Ghare Baire*. But that is an artistic work. If someone wishes to draw good or bad lessons from it then that is not part of the artist's intentions. ...At the time that *Ghare Baire* was written, the writer's likes and dislikes were also woven into it. But those coloured threads were part of his art. If someone wishes to use them for a different purpose then that purpose is the reader's, not the writer's" (*Sabuj Patra* 1916, 520–22).

The social context of *Gora* is quite significant. In my discussion of *Gora,* I have indicated that the kind of nationalism which emerged in Bengal as a result of the Bengal partition and the revolutionary activities that it gave rise to was seriously flawed. Once the excitement had died down, these flaws began to be apparent. Not only did these anomalies become quite clear to Tagore, he also protested against them quite strongly. His own thoughts on nationalism also underwent radical changes as a consequence. In the conflict that seemed to arise between nationalism and humanism, it was the religion of humanism that triumphed in Tagore's consciousness. He was not willing to accept any narrowness in nationalism as separated from humanism. It is important to remember that in this humanist philosophy a very special place was also accorded to individual freedom.

In the first quarter of the twentieth century, there had emerged in Calcutta and in other towns of Bengal a powerful upper middle class. The social ideals of this class had grown around the notions of complete personal independence and humanism. To what extent such ideals helped serve their class interests is a question that is irrelevant to the analysis of the novel. Suffice to say that the conflict that became visible between the ideals and the narrowest form of parochial chauvinism in urban Bengal and that led to such a turmoil in the private and domestic lives of the upper middle-class men and women is the source material for *Ghare Baire.*

It would be a mistake, however, to think of Sandip as the finest example of the main representatives of the Swadeshi Andolan in Bengal. In fact it would also be wrong to assume that the novel gives a complete picture of the Swadeshi Andolan. Like many other major movements, the Swadeshi Andolan also made it possible for some men like Sandip, who were highly intelligent, articulate and yet crudely self-centred and venal, to step out of their ordinary humdrum existence and to explore the opportunities offered by the larger public sphere. Some of these men may have also succeeded in satisfying their base desires by exploiting these opportunities. Similarly, one cannot assume that Nikhilesh represents the entire upper middle class. As I have said earlier, the social ideals of this class were undeniably linked to selfish class interests. But, it would be difficult to detect selfishness even in Nikhilesh's unconscious. His sense of personal autonomy is very high, and it is inspired by the greater ideal of humanism. In order to fulfil this ideal in his own life, he does not hesitate to experiment with his wife Bimala and is willing to take on the suffering that this brings about. One does not ordinarily see this kind of dedication and commitment to ideals in the daily lives of the upper class. Nikhilesh is deeply idealistic. In fact he is so idealistic and other-worldly that his philosophy and beliefs seem to be out of touch with the realities of the world. Despite this, the reason he has not turned pallid and bland in the text is only because of his internal conflicts. The pain that he suffers on account of Bimala and the dilemmas that tear him apart also protect him from this consequence.

There is nothing much to say about the characters of *Ghare Baire.* The particular style of narration that the writer has adopted in this novel has led to the characters' analysing themselves in a fairly adequate manner. In fact Nikhilesh even analyses the flaws in his own idealism in relation to Bimala.

Like Chandranath Babu, Nikhilesh also believes in a certain ideology and ideal, and his life is governed by the efforts to consolidate them. Even while sitting alone during moments of self-reflection when he is excited and moved by his own emotions, he is not shaken for a moment from his ideals. Even during his great mental struggles over Bimala he does not attempt to control her or hold her back. It is as if he is merely an objective viewer and does not even reveal the passions that such spectators sometimes show. After the theft of the coins when he is reunited with Bimala he seems largely detached and rather lifeless.

The same thing can be said about Chandranath Babu. As a character in the novel, his only meaningful role is to help define Nikhilesh more clearly and to give his character some support. He is idealistic like Nikhilesh and he often gives a clearer shape to Nikhilesh's idealism. Whenever Nikhilesh has been unable to analyse his own actions, the need for Chandranath Babu arises.

The most complete characters in *Ghare Baire* are Sandip and Bimala. While Sandip's character is, at a glance, somewhat stricken by his ideology, with Bimala that is not the case. The fullest expression of life takes place through Bimala. Sandip has immense power and also the skill to use it artfully, but he has a worthless character. The Sandip to whom Bimala is attracted is revealed gradually and skilfully. He first beckons her openly and courteously for help with the nation's cause, then goes on to add sound and fury to his call, and finally turns it into an offer of love. Eventually, his mask slips, his greed and crassness are exposed, and in the Amulya episode, his internal weaknesses are completely revealed to Bimala through the cracks made by his jealousy. For the first time then in his life he is struck by what he has done and begins gradually to fear defeat. This does not escape Bimala's gaze either. Before his final exit, we see Sandip's pride and arrogance becoming pale and restricted. But despite that, one has to marvel at the consummate skill with which the writer has kept Sandip's character unchanged till the end and has not allowed his pride and self-esteem to be completely reduced to rubble. Nor does one see traces of contrition in him. The character of Sandip also has other special qualities. He is a "magician with ideas". He can dress his ideas and arguments with such finesse that his fascinating eloquence sometimes outstrips the inadequacies of his character. However, when he argues with Nikhilesh, it is quite clear that his words are untouched by any genuine heart-felt passions. Similarly his exchanges and relations with Bimala are unaffected by emotions. If he had indeed been able to love Bimala deeply and his greed had not been of such a gross variety, then it would have been very difficult to predict what course the events of this novel would have taken. In this novel, Bimala is the most lively character. In the environment in which she has been shaped, the husband is the only man of importance within the kingdom of conjugal relations. The sphere of freedom within which Nikhilesh wants to love her seems to have no use for her; in fact one doubts whether she even understands the significance of her husband's ideals. But, when the waves of the Swadeshi Andolan rush in through the open doors of Nikhilesh's house and strike its inner quarters, she is swept outside and brought face to face with Sandip. Caught in the passion that the andolan arouses in her, she fails to see the real Sandip and views him instead as a strong and dedicated worker determined to break the shackles binding his motherland. The manner in which she then gradually reveals herself to Sandip begins to find her husband Nikhilesh weak in comparison to him, causes her to distance herself from Nikhilesh as she becomes increasingly infatuated with Sandip, and is even tempted to give in to Sandip's lust—all of this is gradually developed in the novel. Subsequently, one begins to see hesitation and uncertainty in Sandip while Nikhilesh's unyielding idealism begins to enfeeble him from within. Towards the end, Sandip's ugly avarice and intemperance are brought out in the open over the matter of the money, and Bimala becomes completely disenchanted with him, and, finally, when he attempts to draw her into his arms she spurns him with disgust and hatred. When his unabashed and base venality are thus exposed, Bimala's efforts become solely directed to freeing herself from the clutches of her infatuation and that is when the need for Amulya arises. She draws strength from the maternal affection he arouses in her heart, and she uses this traditional form of love to save herself from the path to destruction. On her way to disillusionment, while Bimala frequently expresses guilt and sorrow, it is clear that this guilt is not so much for the loss of Nikhilesh's love as it is for the shame over the theft and for having sent Amulya to his death. That she realises the true significance of Nikhilesh's ideals and that she returns to the hearth on the basis of such a realisation are nowhere indicated in the narrative. Bimala does, however, understand that she had only received Nikhilesh's love without giving anything in return and that therefore her love is weak. Nikhilesh also realises that there was an element of force in his ideal of love. However, there is nothing in the narrative to suggest that they are brought closer to each other with greater intensity and strength as a result of their tumultuous experiences in the world. Bimala it seems returns in order to save her position and dignity and the traditional honour of the family, to protect herself from the insinuations of Mejorani, and, above all, because of her overpowering love for Amulya. The fact that she does not express any particular anxiety or concern when Nikhilesh returns in the end, injured and dying, only helps to strengthen this suspicion.

But, the character who despite her restricted representation is the most life-like is Mejorani. At one level she is a jealous woman; her jealousy is directed towards Bimala's fortunes which is quite understandable given Nikhilesh's family traditions and the contemporary context. This jealousy, however, also gives her a keen, incisive vision owing to which and a woman's natural instinct she is able to discern without any great difficulty the meaning and intent of Bimala's careful self-adornment, her mannerisms, and wiles. Besides, there is no use denying that her affection for Nikhilesh is not entirely unalloyed by a certain degree of physical desire for him. At another level, however, at the time when Sandip and Nikhilesh are engaged in their bitter battles, Mejorani's jealous rage against Bimala is transformed into anxious concern and sympathy for her brother-in-law, and her physical desire is transformed into affectionate care and the urgency to create a refuge for him. The sweet tenderness and friendship that had flowered between them in their childhood and that had subsequently been scarred by jealousy and unfulfilled desires are retrieved once again and the very possibility of Bimala's infidelity leads Mejorani to become Nikhilesh's companion in his moments of acute agony and to cocoon him with her sympathetic concern.

One has to, however, express one reservation regarding *Ghare Baire*. The problem falls within the purview of literary analysis, even though it seems to arise out of a concern with social issues. The problem in fact has been created by the writer himself. Through Nikhilesh, the writer has attempted to create a certain ideal of conjugal relations. Nikhilesh wishes to seek Bimala within an autonomous space and not through the easy exercise of his traditional and socially sanctioned rights as a husband. He was firmly determined to earn her love within the competition made possible by the outer world. It is in the pursuit of this ideal that Bimala is thrust into the struggles and challenges of the outer world. But then is Sandip, the other man in this field of competition, a genuinely worthy adversary to Nikhilesh? The Swadeshi Andolan had snatched many a man from their protected lives and freed them for a public existence. While it is true that of these some may have had the philosophy and reasoning of Sandip, it is also equally true that not all of them were avaricious and crudely materialistic like him. Given the manner in which the writer has created the course of events, it would have been quite possible for one such person to have come before Bimala and to have loved her deeply. Who can say what the problem then would have led to? In his relations with Bimala, Sandip's emotions remain untouched, for he only desires her for his physical pleasures. Had he loved her sincerely, would not the novel have taken a different path altogether? Therefore, it seems as though the writer having put forth a problem, then fails to explore it adequately; the sphere of conflict does not quite live up to the problem. Besides, the manner in which Bimala is made to return fails to mark the triumph of Nikhilesh's ideal of love. The truth is that the yardstick used to judge this ideal is not a fair one. Sandip has not been created as Nikhilesh's worthy adversary. The reader continues to be haunted by the question that had he not been portrayed as so base and limited an individual, how would the characters have emerged from their trials.

Notes

1. The present chapter is a translation by the editors of certain excerpts from a chapter from Prof Niharranjan Ray's critical work in Bangla on Tagore's literary writings titled, *Rabindra Sahityer Bhumika* (*The Role of Rabindranath Tagore's Literature*), Calcutta, New Age Publishers Private Limited, 1962, 397–435.

HOME/ *GHARE*

3

Andare Antare/Inner Worlds[1]

SAMBUDDHA CHAKRABARTI

Ghare Baire was serialised in 1915; as a novel it was published the next year, in 1916. The events narrated in the novel belong to an earlier decade. In the history of undivided Bengal, this period is widely familiar as the era of 'bangabhanga' (the partition of Bengal) and the swadeshi movement.

The partition of Bengal and the subsequent boycott and swadeshi movements represent the political context of *Ghare Baire*. The opinions and debates surrounding the boycott and the swadeshi movements—the contradictions and the conflicts—inform, rather obviously, the novel. The three leading characters of *Ghare Baire*, Nikhilesh, Bimala, and Sandip appear against the hinterland of this central, historical event. Bimala's first appearance may be as Nikhilesh's wife, but later she too gets involved with the movement and even though her participation is not a direct one, her activities behind the scene represent a crucial element of the novel.

Ghare Baire also has a social context. The novel's political background is obvious and manifests itself evidently. The swadeshi movement is an accepted and widely discussed chapter in the Indian history of nationalism. It can therefore be easily recognised by the readers of the novel. In comparative terms, it is not so easy to grasp the social context of the novel which was an evolving history of the last few decades of the nineteenth century. *Baire*—the outside world's revolution is shaped by obvious and immediate political will; but behind the changes, in the *ghar*—the private world of the home—lie the mutating attitudes of more than half a century. Actually, a quiet change inside the home is introduced to the readers much before they confront the political events in the novel. It is this change at home that enables the confluence of the home and the world, making the novel possible.

Bimala inhabited the antahpur—the secluded inner quarters of the house—like many other housewives in Bengal, with of course one difference: Bimala was a zamindar's wife. This Bimala, who knew herself only as a housewife, is encouraged by her husband, Nikhilesh, to take her first step outside the secluded private chamber, shedding her initial hesitations, embarrassments, and inhibitions. Bimala from the antahpur, hitherto surrounded by close relatives and domestic hands, comes to the public quarters of the home and gets to know her husband's friend, Sandip. This is the preface to the rest of the novel, but to see it only in this light is to miss the significance of this movement. Bimala's appearance in the public chambers of the house, outside the secluded world of the antahpur, might appear to be rather easy but in reality it was a far more complex and fraught process.

I

The influence of Western education and philosophy on the traditional and custom-driven society of Bengal starts manifesting itself from the second and third decades of the nineteenth century. Initially confined to a few students and Western-educated men, this influence proliferated alongside the spread of education. An inevitable effect of this was the comparison of the Bengali and the Western social institutions, leading to an evaluation of one's own culture, customs, rules and regulations. In this comparative evaluation of the Western and Bengali social systems, the social position of Bengali women was foregrounded as the chief evidence of the latter's backwardness, and attempts were made to correct this. Thus, of all the debates and agitations about the social reforms of the nineteenth century, the majority centred on those that dealt with women's utter helplessness and position in society. Sati, child marriage, the incongruous age difference between bride and groom, the condition of widows, polygamy etc., become critical social issues. After centuries of indifference and contempt, women emerged from behind the scene as the focus of debate and discussion.

The Bengali men who were the recipients of a Western education soon felt the need to educate their wives as well. During this period of actual growth of female education, there were doubts and debates over the importance and propriety of female education, the subjects that they should study, the place where this knowledge should be imparted etc., as well as the absolute antagonism of the conservative section of society. But as the century progressed, the degree of hostility lessened. The question of equal right to education for men and women never arose in the nineteenth century, but towards the close of the century the belief that women should not be educated at all was on the decline. Few agreed, however, that women should be educated on par with the men. Instead, what gradually acquired acceptance was the notion of an education specially oriented for women and a new word was coined: "*strijanochita shikhya*", that is, an education fit for women. A related corollary was the belief that women should not be confined to the antahpur. Journals and periodicals, published specifically for women, started appearing from the second half of the nineteenth century. The improvement in the condition of the women, their breaking free of and stepping out of the antahpur, female education, the running of the household and the cataloguing of various ethical feminine virtues were the main subjects of these publications.

As the nineteenth century drew to a close, yet another manifestation of the changing times was the emerging belief that women should not only acquire the required education but also become able companions, though in a limited sense, of their husbands. *Ghare Baire*'s Nikhilesh represents this conviction. He desires that Bimala should step out of the confined world of the antahpur. He cites his reason thus: "I want that you should find me, and I find you, in the world outside. Our exchange in the world outside remains." Nikhilesh's argument for not confining his wife within the antahpur is that she should, "...Come out into the world for once and understand it for yourself. You were not meant to be confined to the chores of a deceiving notion of the home, any more than I am. Our love can be fulfilled only if our identities mature amidst truth."[2]

Certainly, not every educated man wanted to bring women to the world outside the home. But a section emerged that believed that they should be brought out, and this section swelled gradually. A corresponding manifestation of change in women was also inevitable. The newly enlightened women became far more confident and aware, though initially their numbers, too, were few. The women's discourse in several stories and novels of the first two decades of the twentieth century, which is often the language of protest, could not have occurred in the nineteenth century. Mrinal, the protagonist of *Strir Patra* (The Letter from a Wife), is a product of the twentieth century. What she does would not have been possible in the previous century. The social progress that takes place occurs very slowly, almost imperceptibly.

We need to know the daily routine of a woman's life in the antahpur of a nineteenth-century Bengali household in order to acquire a perspective on this transformation and to understand the critical significance of the Bengali woman's debut in the public world. Though this does not represent Bimala's household, a familiarity with the daily life of the ordinary Bengali *bhadramahila* would help us understand the nineteenth-century "home" from which she emerges.

II

Bengali society still condemned the practice of women venturing outside their homes even though the previous century's strictures of confining women to the private quarters of the house were getting gradually relaxed. This attitude continued to frustrate the growth of female education in the nineteenth-century. The household occupied virtually the entire existence of a woman's life. A history of the household and the history of women in nineteenth-century Bengal are thus almost inseparable.

The main problems of emplotting the history of women in the nineteenth century also apply to the project of historicising the household. There are no documented records of the household for future reference. Documents imprisoned in official files or evidence from archeological remains are not of much help in scripting the history of the household. It therefore needs to be gleaned from contemporary literature, articles that appeared in the various journals, and letters. From these, a collage of life of nineteenth-century Bengali society emerges, depicting women's daily lives and household duties, the marital home, and the compulsions of life in a joint family. From material thus gathered, however, a precise image of the age cannot be constructed; but the historian studying nineteenth-century households has no other data to work with.

Nineteenth-century society ordained very early marriages for girls. Thus, when we talk of the household for women, the reference is to their marital homes which may signify the husband's house and/or the marital joint household. In either case, it represents the post-marriage state for women. A woman's brief life in her natal home as a child may thus be described as merely a preparation for her "real" life after marriage. A major feature of the education received by girls before marriage also foregrounded this belief. In 1903, Sarojini Devi writes in the journal, *Antahpur*, that, "The mothers who impart to their daughters a knowledge of housework, arts and crafts, cooking, the upbringing of children, care for the ailing, the well being of others, thrift, piety, respect, mercy, courtesy and above all religious education in order to improve their social, ethical and philosophical endeavours and make easy their future roles as good mothers and good wives, are the ideal mothers."[3] Numerous articles in the periodicals and journals of the period also reiterate the social belief that a woman's "true" life is spent in her marital home.

In Bankimchandra Chattopadhyay's novel, *Indira,* (1873), the eponymous protagonist describes the marital household to her sister Kamini thus: "That's the cupid's garden, there the god of love impales the heart with arrows of flower and gratifies one's existence. On stepping there a woman becomes an *apsara*, a voluptuous celestial nymph, and the men lambs. There the *Koel* sings daily, the south wind blows in winter and the full moon rises during *amavasya,* the dark phase of the new moon."[4] A picture of fulfilment rises before the reader's eye, but does not the obvious exaggeration signify a sharp satire? Why else would Kamini, at the end of this alluring description, pinch her elder sister's cheek and say, "Like death or what?", an idiomatic expression that really means, "tell me another". Is this description then entirely ironical?

III

Women's roles in nineteenth-century Bengali society was usually divided into three segments: daughter, wife, and mother. Of these, the phase of "daughter" was brief as early marriages hurried the girls into the marital households where they spent their remaining lives as "wife" and "mother". Within these two expansive appellations was the embrace of several other relationships that women had to observe all through their lives because of the demanding structure of the family. The new child-wife entrant to a joint family was not just the "wife" of a single individual. She was the daughter-in-law of her husband's parents as well as of their contemporaries. She was also the sister-in-law of her husband's siblings. In later years, through motherhood, she would graduate to being an in-law herself. Each of these relationships had a claim on the woman, and the bonds of these relationships were much stronger than they are today. After her marriage at the age of 10–12 years, the rest of a woman's life revolved about these relationships.[5] In the context of the nineteenth century thus, the marital home signified a fine web of several relationships. During the wedding (or in several cases in later years as well), the relationship with the husband was quite insignificant; the bride's relationship with the other members of the marital household was often of much greater importance.

Evicted from the mother's lap, the nineteenth-century child-bride's most significant relationship as "wife" was with the mother-in-law. On reading contemporary writings, however, one feels that this relationship was hardly one of maternal affection and care. An article in the journal, *Bangamahila,* contours this relationship thus: "Most mothers-in-law do not consider their son's wives to be anything but their own maid servants. Most married men are acquainted with the following ritual question and answer exchanged between the groom and his mother on the eve of his departure for the wedding ceremony: the mother asks, 'What are you going to bring ?'. 'A maid for you, mother' is the son's answer."[6]

The writer of this article, written in 1875, recalls this ritualised promise of the son not only because it was seen as traditional behaviour but also because, in the nineteenth century, the wife's life was circumscribed by the all-encompassing authority of the mother-in-law. The antahpur was the field of a woman's domineering influence, despite her position in society vis-à-vis men. The lady of the household, henceforth referred to as the *grihini*, possessed absolute power within this limited territory: "As the king in a country and a zamindar in a village, thus is the grihini in a Bengali household. The power of the king and the zamindar is still limited as from time to time they need to be apprehensive of their wives. But the grihini or *ginni* has boundless power. She has great authority."[7] This comparison of the lady of the household with a feudal seat of power is not an isolated one. Numerous articles of the period compare the grihini to the king or the zamindar to help explain the extent of her power.[8]

It is, however, not enough to say that the grihini possessed absolute power within the family. The structure of the Bengali joint family was such that while there was only one male head, known as the *karta*, there could be many grihinis. Other than the wife of the karta, often more than one elderly lady were part of the

Bengali joint family owing to financial or other compulsions, "These *kartris* or grihinis have a conspicuous presence in Bengal as maternal or paternal aunts, grandmothers, and widowed elder sisters."[9] They too wielded enormous power within the antahpur. The new bride's happiness and fate depended upon all these ladies. We will club the mother-in-law and these other ladies of the joint family who would be her contemporaries in the same category of "grihini" in our critical study of the household.

In an essay titled, 'Nababadhu' (The New Bride), published in the journal, *Antahpur* (1902), Hiranmayi Sengupta describes the new bride's situation: "There is a tradition of child marriage in our Hindu families and so the bride is of a tender age. If she is treated kindly from the beginning and as one's own offspring, then the bride likewise could become a daughter, but it is a matter of great regret that in most families the bride is mercilessly tormented."[10] An anonymous essayist in the journal *Bangamahila* (1875) notes in a criticism that the brides are not only treated as maids but that the "Grihinis passed a decree that the acts of speaking and unveiling of the brides' heads and faces are to be censured", even though the maid servants of the households do not need to keep their heads and faces veiled.[11] Of course, the bride could please the mother-in-law by obeying "all orders just or unjust" quietly and by working hard like a domestic help, as only then could she be the ideal daughter-in-law in the eyes of the lady of the household and earn the appellation of "Lakshmi bou", a wife like the Hindu goddess Lakshmi associated with prosperity and conjugal fulfilment.[12] Otherwise she would become an object of displeasure for the mother-in-law—not a very happy experience for the bride, particularly in the context of her lack of intimacy with the husband. Evidently, this kind of relationship between the mother-in-law and the daughter-in-law was not confined to a few stray incidents: "It is as though the chief task of the mother-in-law is to torment the daughter-in-law over unimportant and minute household details."[13] This oppressive state of affairs for the bride in the marital household remained largely unaltered over a long time.

An important leitmotif in the discussions of the social reformers of the nineteenth century was the neglected status of women in society. But in these discussions, women were always located in terms of their difference from men. The stratification of women themselves in ensuring familial control was thus not addressed. In a patriarchal society, women have to accept male domination, but the suppressed female ego also tries to acquire fulfilment in accordance to its status in the antahpur. Its easiest target in the nineteenth-century household was the daughter-in-law. Her deportment, speech, work—every aspect of her existence—was a subject of critical appraisal of the family's presiding lady. Satiprakash Sen's description (1880) of the state of the new bride is precise and critical: "The new bride is always guilty and at fault. Her gait, eating habits, cooking, speech, gestures are all found wanting. If she is hungry she cannot say so, or eat till her hunger's abated, she cannot express any desire or cry when she is berated, she cannot mention that she is ill, cannot laugh and speak, can not show that she is tormented."[14] This oppressive existence may not have applied to every family, but certainly this was the norm for the daughters-in-law of the majority of the families. Satiprakash Sen's description of the new bride's life concludes thus: "This is the norm for the Bengali family, the tradition of the Bengali household and the prized custom of the Bengali society... The bride is guilty on all counts, if she walks fast then she is saucy, if she walks slowly then she is lazy, if she laughs she is shameless, proud if she does not laugh, if she talks she is garrulous, arrogant if she does not, if she eats when hungry then she is an ogress, if she does not then she is described as being contemptuous... The bride is exempted from all earthly happiness".[15] Other than these general social observations it is also possible to locate a couple of actual instances from the pages of family chronicles of the nineteenth century. The journal, *Paricarika* (1891), describes the torturing of a daughter-in-law by her mother-in-law of the renowned *raj* family of Shobhabazar. The latter did not allow her daughter-in-law to eat or wear clothes of her choice. The woman's husband did not protest against his mother's behaviour either. In fact, in most cases, the mothers-in-law could take advantage of the lack of intimacy between the husband and the wife to establish domination over the bride. The essayist of *Paricarika* comments that, "It is a matter of national shame and embarrassment that such an unfortunate incident took place in a renowned and respectable family of a gentleman."[16]

Despite the expressed surprise of *Paricarika*, even extremely "progressive" families did not always refrain from this oppressive treatment of daughters-in-law. Satyendranath Tagore's wife, Jnanadanandini Devi, perhaps did not have a very happy relationship with her mother-in-law. We learn from her memoirs that she would often be scolded by her mother-in-law because of what the maids of the house reported.[17] Perhaps this worried Satyendranath Tagore also. In a letter dated 26 February 1864, he enquires from London: "Does ma talk to you at times or does she stay aloof, as earlier?"

On reading the nineteenth-century writings, it does appear that the elderly ladies managed to gratify, to some extent, the crushed egos of lives spent entirely in the patriarchal enclosure by establishing authority over the young daughters-in-law. But such gratification was not available to the daughters-in-law. An inevitable consequence of this exertion of power was the silent immersion of the daughter-in-law in ceaseless household chores. A description by Harihar Sheth of the young wife's routine household work notes that "The family may have ten members, but only the ailing adolescent or young wife will be working in the kitchen for their meals twice a day in the terrible heat. Some members of the family will have to go to school, some to the office, some will refuse to eat before two in the afternoon...and in between working out their conveniences she will have to keep an eye on her small children or pay attention to her husband's request even as she completes the other household chores. Yet leave alone any words of sympathy the mother-in-law will always sulk and from time to time torment her with harsh words...Now a days there are many such wealthy households where there is no paucity of money, Landau cars and toadies a plenty and no expenses spared for religious festivals, marriages or parties. Yet there are no proper woollens to protect the young bride's ailing body in winter, no adequate treatment for her ailment, not enough maids for the housework and not even the provision for the required amount of milk for her."[18] The journal *Bamabodhini Patrika* in 1887 called this kind of behaviour with the daughters-in-law, "*badhushashan*" or the disciplining of wives.[19]

Sharp rebukes and extracted labour apart, another easy way for the mothers-in-law to establish their authority over the daughters-in-law was to disallow their visits to their natal homes. This was considered to be one of the several ways in which a displeased mother-in-law could "punish" her son's wife. If the gifts given during the wedding or the dowry were not to the liking of the groom's family, the child-bride had to pay a price for her parents' crime. It would be ordained then that she was not to visit her parents.[20] The number of brides who had to sever ties with their natal homes on the directive of the marital homes is not negligible. In the novel *Yugantar* (first published, 1894), Bhubaneswari, the daughter of the protagonist Vishwanath Tarkabhushan, is disciplined thus by her mother-in-law, who is displeased with the bride's family: "Come child, enter the house and never mention visiting your father's house ever again."[21] Bhubaneswari is not allowed to visit her natal home for the next three years.[22] In Rabindranath Tagore's short story, *Dena Paona,* the protagonist, Nirupama, is slighted by her in-laws primarily because of her father's inability to give the promised amount of money.[23] In yet another short story, *Haimanti* (1914), written later by Tagore, Haimanti's in-laws also refuse to let her visit her natal home as part of the punishment meted out to her.

Motherhood signalled an enhanced status of a daughter-in-law within the family. This attitude prevailed not just in the ordinary Bengali families but even in the extremely progressive ones. Jnanadanandini Devi, a daughter-in-law of the Tagore family, had written in her memoirs that, "I was made much of when I first came to the house with my two sons. There would not have been much affection in the absence of sons. There is no warmth for a barren wife."[24] The daughter-in-law acquired greater power with motherhood. She no longer suffered her mother-in-law without protesting.[25] The long-suppressed anger could then manifest itself. Rajanikanta Gupta writes in 1907 that, "Quite often the verbal battle between the mother-in-law and the daughter-in-law would transform into a physical one."[26] The ignominies suffered at the hands of the mother-in-law would be further compensated once the bride herself became the grihini of the household. Thus turned the wheel in Bengali society for each generation of women; from accepting authority in the marital home to maintaining and perpetuating that authority as, "This is how the role of the grihini has traditionally carried on."[27]

Even though virtually every bride had to accept authoritarian behaviour when young, not every bride was ill treated by the mother-in-law. Rasasundari Devi in her autobiography has expressed gratitude for the compassionate behaviour of her mother-in-law: "I was made much of at my father's house....Later I went as a new bride to a new place but here too affection was not wanting, in fact it increased. My mother-in-law used to get many toys for me. She used to ask all the other girls of the village to come and meet me."[28] Kailashbashini Devi (1828–95) has not written about sour relations with the mother-in-law either. The incidents that she mentions, such as sleeping with her mother-in-law at night,[29] lead one to assume that they had a cordial relationship. Prafullamoyee (1852–1940), wife of Debendranath Tagore's younger brother, Birendranath, respected her mother-in-law and was loved by her in return. She wrote on the death of her mother-in-law that, "She has left assuaging everyone's sorrow and need with great dexterity. She never tried to hurt anyone through deprivation."[30] This statement of course needs to be taken with a pinch of salt, for it was know that there was an insurmountable wall between Debendranath Tagore's wife, Sarada Devi, and one of her daughters-in-law, Jnanadanandini Devi. On the other hand Prasannamoyee Devi (1857–1939), who visited her in-law's house only thrice in her entire life, received love and affection. She also mentions that her mother-in-law would sharply rebuke the villagers who would gather around the educated, chemise- and jacket-clad new bride and pass sharp comments. But the daughter-in-law too would be corrected in private.[31] In the nineteenth century, examples of mothers-in law trying to protect the new bride from the critics are rare. In fact the picture that emerges is the exact opposite. The mothers-in-law were only too ready to chastise the daughters-in-law.[32] The little evidence of an amiable relationship between the mother-in-law and the daughter-in-law are all from personal memoirs. On the other hand, innumerable articles bear testimony to the slights that the daughters-in-law suffered at the hands of the mothers-in-law. This attitude towards the daughter-in-law was also cited as the tradition of Bengali families.

There was more to the lives of the brides at the marital households other than persecution and the wretchedness suffered at the hands of their mothers-in-law. Endless work would also be given to them. The dominant anxiety from the late nineteenth century was that female education might shake and destroy the prevalent social system. The contradictory desires to transform society and yet preserve male domination lay at the root of entrusting women with work that was feminised and thereby held special. The same anxiety compelled many contemporary articles to prove the importance of housework in female lives. As a result, women were feted as "Griha-Lakshmi", the Hindu presiding deity of the household, in the same age that heralded female education: "Truth to tell, familial happiness depends far more on the womankind. It is a woman's duty to adorn and grace the home."[33] The practice of the division of labour into private and public realms helped extol feminine work: "What the kingdom is to the king, the family is to a woman. The family is the arena of her sovereignty. Here the woman is responsible for regulating everyone's happiness and well being and also for executing all household duties judiciously."[34] But the encomiums also ensured that the woman could continue to be heaped with work.

This argument that the family is a woman's priority was also voiced by women themselves. The theory of male self-interest alone cannot explain this, for if this is male propaganda for keeping women housebound, then why was it also voiced by women? Yet, that which appears to be incoherent in the realm of reason is often manifested in the real world. Women nurtured within patriarchy would "naturally" have a patriarchal consciousness. Moreover, the families of the bhadralok in nineteenth-century Bengal had a special structural distinction: the control and stratification of power in the antahpur was two-tiered. In most cases the stratification was in terms of the hierarchy of age. Women of advanced age thus lent their voice to the male choric argument for confining women to the family and for the traditional control of familial power, despite their unequal position and marginalisation in society as women, since they occupied the powered position in the antahpur. These factors, a patriarchal outlook and a fear of loss of power within the given system, ensured that women voiced male speech. In several cases, unless the name was mentioned, it was difficult to make out the gender of the author as they exhorted the importance of household duties in female lives. Feminine work in the household was iconised and put on a pedestal as Bengal's traditional and cultural heritage. Rasasundari Devi's autobiography also recognises this circumscribing of female life, "Women will work in the house, will cook, will be modest, this is what we know."[35]

Just as the men were apprehensive about female education and wanted to contain the project within a defined ambit, similarly the elderly ladies in control of the family also expressed anxiety about female education which might lead to familial control passing into the hands of the newly educated women. This fear was also openly admitted in an article published in the journal *Bamabodhini Patrika*: "They (the educated Bengali women) instead of respecting their husbands often express sharp, impertinent and cruel statements. They try and control the mother-in-law and other elders with great discourtesy. They waste their time in purposeless amusements such as playing cards instead of paying attention to the housework."[36] The same article also comments that the ladies of Bengal were evolving into "symbols of selfishness". This was written in the year 1874. Thirty-two years later, the same anxiety is expressed in another article in language extremely forthright and unambiguous: "The girls are educated in the school for *Bibi*s, some learn English art and craft and some acquire expertise in painting and music. Virtually all neglect cooking and housework, profess contempt for the reading of religious texts and observation of the religious rituals."[37] Clearly the dominant anxiety was that the newly educated woman would be unmindful and lax in two areas: household work and religious duties.

The letters and the journals of the nineteenth century, while discussing female life, have not indicated the differences between city and suburbs. A comparison between the city and the mofussils may lead one to assume a liberal and free environment of the former, but that would largely be either imaginary or a case of assuming that the antahpur was also transformed in keeping with the outside environment. Chitra Dev has observed that life for women in the city was actually far more confined: "In the village the women would have ponds with crystal clear water, they could step on the carpet of grass, lift their heads and see the sun in the blue sky. The city had none of these. Screens, curtains, small windows, blinds were all around the women. They were prohibited from going to the corridors outside the house, or to go up to the open terrace and there was no question of their stepping outside the threshold of the house."[38] The antahpur in the city was hardly an arena of freedom. In fact, in several writings of the period, where housework is being described, it is difficult to make out whether the protagonist is from the city or a suburb unless it is specifically mentioned. There was also perhaps not much variation in the lives of the women across the ordinary households of Kolkata.

There was, however, a difference in the lifestyles of the Brahmo and non-Brahmo families. In Bengal, the spread of female education was the most in the Brahmo families that played a leading role in the debates over the position of women in the nineteenth century. The primary difference apparent in the lives of women in Brahmo and non-Brahmo families is a difference in the consciousness of life—a delicate taste manifesting itself in the daily lifestyle. In the daily routine itself though, the Brahmo-non-Brahmo difference was only a marginal one. In the nineteenth century, as in every other period, the primary index of lifestyle was the financial status. A certain degree of similarity was apparent in the lifestyles of families who were culturally and financially alike, but may have been living in different places. There was a world of difference, however, between the lives of the wives of the rich and of the middle-class families living in the same city of Kolkata.

IV

A favourable environment for encouraging the growth of conjugal closeness did not exist even in the first half of the nineteenth century. The husband and wife could not meet during the day. The reason for this was not the husband's work pressure or a deliberate neglect of the wife on his part. In the social and familial value systems of the period, meetings between the husband and wife during the day were condemned. Reverend Lal Behari Dey observed that, "...in this country women do not get any chance to speak to their husbands in peace except at night. They are engaged in kitchen and housework during the day and even when they get a respite they are too embarrassed to either sit or converse with the husbands. The young woman who converses with the husband during the day is considered to be a loose woman by the neighbours, especially the old ladies."[39] As married couples could meet only at night, the kind of conjugal love that grew up between the two needs no elaboration. This taboo on the meeting of the husband and wife during the course of the day carried well into the nineteenth century. Even after three-fourths of the century had rolled by, we find a satire in which the mother-in-law holds the daughter-in-law guilty of the crime of talking to her husband during the day: "My goodness! I have never seen such a shameless hussy in the whole wide world. She is so unrestrained in chatting with her husband. O shame! Even with one foot in the grave I still feel embarrassed to look him (her husband) in the eye and talk. My oh my, what has the world come to! After all this is the age of *Kali*![40] From where did he get a whore's daughter for our family?... there is not a jot of shame."[41]

We have already marked Reverend Lal Behari Dey's observation in *Chandramukhir Upakhyan* that daylight encounters between husbands and wives were held in great shame. In a book written much later we gather from the conversation between the husband and the wife on the wedding night that this social outlook had not changed much. When the first night of their conjugal life is spent in talking and the dawn breaks, the husband says to the wife: "What! It's already morning. See how awful is the custom of the country. If you did not have to be veiled during the day then would there be this bother of staying up through the night? You need not be so embarrassed in the daytime, let people be critical, it doesn't matter to us."[42] A free conjugal relationship cannot evolve in a society that is critical of conjugal encounters in the light of day. A signed letter, "Younger Sister", published in the journal *Paricharika*, expressed a female resolve in 1879 that: "I will never marry, but die an old maid, unless I see married girls more happy with their husbands."[43]

Polygamy, child marriage or the wide gulf in age—whatever be the reason—there was often a kind of distance between the husband and the wife. At times, the gulf was mental and emotional, and at times, physical. Where the physical relationship is wanting we find enough evidence of male waywardness. But female dissatisfaction was also expressed in myriad ways. But even if some women were inclined to seek sexual gratification outside marriage, most spent their lifetime in immeasurable grief and nursed a hatred for the irresponsible husband. Despite the proliferation of long-drawn out published advice on wifely duties in the nineteenth century, a majority of wives deprived of their husband's company held them guilty all their lives even as they blamed their own fate as long as they lived.

The conversation of two sisters in Tarakchandra Churamani's play *Sapatni Natak* (1857) makes clear how openly this pain of separation could reveal itself. Nitambini and Chanchala are both wives of *kulin* families. They do not meet their husbands. Nitambini's speech reveals the frustrated desires of women, both psychological and physical: "A man has fifty, sixty or even a hundred wives. Let him ruin himself by roaming about with a staff and a pot....What's the point in complaining to father after we have fallen into the hands of a greedy, senile addict? My life is ruined and there is no hope of salvation in the next life either, sister." On hearing this, the reply of Chanchala to her elder sister Kadambini, is even more suggestive, "*Didi*! Did you hear that? Nitu seems to be in a state of frenzy, the fire in her has been kindled, she can't be at peace. Oh my! It is difficult to recognize her."[44]

It is not as though these problems such as polygamy, child marriage, wide age difference between the bride and the groom, female illiteracy, etc., that crucially affected the lives of women were new issues in the latter half of the nineteenth century. They had been part of Bengali society for a long time. But from the latter half of the nineteenth century, people were becoming conscious of the evil effects of these customs upon society, as can be gathered from the dates of the quoted articles of the period. This does not mean, however, that all those who started writing were either "social reformers" or "progressive".

V

Despite the difficulties and hurdles placed in the way of evolving a more companionate conjugal relationship, the newly educated young men of the nineteenth century felt inspired enough by the liberal environment and ideas of the period to fancy an intellectual and emotional companion in the wife. This was not possible without educating her. The conservatives were content with the older conjugal and familial relationships. But this did not dissuade the newly educated young men from their efforts to educate their wives for the purpose of companionship. The clash over female education between the conservative and the progressive is rooted in this difference.

Prassannakumar Tagore's son Jnanendramohan Tagore strove to make his wife "modern" in the context of this period—in fact he even appointed an English governess for the proper education of his wife.[45] Satyendranath Tagore, while in England, used to enquire about his wife through letters. He requested his brother Hemendranath Tagore (Debendranath Tagore's younger brother, next in line to Satyendranath) to ensure an English education for Jnanadanandini Devi.[46] Girishchandra Sen used to teach his wife, *Barnaparichay*, the elementary introduction to the alphabets, after the rest of the house went to sleep.[47] Kesav Sen's mother, Saradasundari Devi, was always encouraged by her husband, Pyaricharan Sen, to study and he would himself often teach her at night.[48] Sitanath Tattvabhushan (married in 1885, later the president of the Brahmo Samaj) used to teach his wife Nagendrabala Dutta, and his daughter and biographer, Jyotirmoyi Mukhopadhyaya, has written that Sitanath's memoirs prove that he taught his wife everyday.[49]

No one who undertook this enterprise of educating the wife at home harboured the illusion that the wife's knowledge would equal the husband's. Actually in most cases the husband believed and hoped that imparting some education would enable the wife to understand his emotions, ideals, etc., more profoundly. Education was thus the first step towards moulding the wife in the desired manner. The husbands who did not limit themselves to just educating the wives would try to expand their horizon a bit more. Satyendranath was against the *purdah* system and he was in favour of female emancipation. He wanted the women of the household to step into the world outside the home. He couldn't take his wife to England because of the disapproval of his father, Debendranath Tagore, but he did send his wife to a dinner party at the Viceroy's house in 1866.[50]

This new attitude that the wife should not only be a life partner but also an intellectual companion who could share the husband's personal happiness and sorrow is noticeable from the second half of the nineteenth century. The newly acquired value system that made the Bengali conscious of the wife's position in the family also heralded a new notion of conjugality that developed soon into a new feeling of romantic love between married couples. Those who did not keep track of this transformation also failed to understand its importance: it is not that they were unaware of the unhappy condition of women, but they could not free themselves of the traditional moorings of the husband-wife relationship like Sibnath Sastri's father, Debendranath Tagore, or Prassannakumar Tagore. Prassannakumar Tagore was also at the dinner in the Viceroy's house that Jnanadanandini Devi attended. He ran away from there in anger and shame on seeing the daughter-in-law of the family presenting herself before male strangers.[51] The reason was his unfamiliarity with the new thinking.

Contemporary literature bears witness to the development of romantic love that had blossomed and expressed itself alongside all the complexities, hesitation, self-denial, and anguish of Bengali life. This new consciousness can also be observed in some biographies from the same period. The greatest example of the influence of romantic love is in the poem, *Premer Abhishek* or "The Coronation of Romantic love", which expresses the sentiment that the glory of love is such that it exalts and endows with a special meaning even the ordinary lives. This aspect of love was expressed by Rabindranath Tagore in 1893 in the form of a poem. He hailed the victory of love, thus:

> You have made an emperor of me. You have
> Crowned me in glory. Garlands
> You wreathed round my throat, your regal insignia
> Marks my forehead and flames
> Constant incandescence. All my indigence-shame
> All my insignificance is covered today
> By your royal garb.[52]

The clerk whose "grimy", realistic portrait was also drawn by Rabindranath Tagore could proclaim with confidence once he had been emancipated by the rush of romantic love thus :

> I am radiant
> Like the gods with eternal youth,
> There my charms know no bound
> Where your glory abounds
> In the universe of love, there my courtiers
> Are the sun, moon and stars, who in new attire
> Sing to me songs evermore new,
> Endowed with new meanings—a constant ally
> Everywhere.[53]

The tremors evoked by "songs evermore new", and "Endowed with new meaning", stirred the hearts of Bengalis of the nineteenth century. But when we see the manifestation of this love in Bengali life and literature, it is difficult to believe that this new ideal was distanced from the majority of lives in Bengali society.

The Brahmo Samaj allowed greater social intercourse between men and women in contrast to Hindu society. While the latter was still critical of allowing women to appear before men other than the family, the Brahmo Samaj was far more relaxed. As a result, a bride and groom from the Brahmo Samaj had more of an opportunity to get to know each other prior to marriage. Sudakshina Sen's husband, Ambikacharan Sen, for instance, even spent the night at the Dhaka residence of Sudakhshina where the negotiation of their marriage was being settled.[54] The two daughters of Kesavchandra Sen, Suniti and Sucharu, also married men they knew before marriage, even though they did not belong to the Brahmo Samaj. Satyendranath Tagore and Jnanadanandini Devi's daughter, Indira Devi, married Pramath Chaudhuri with whom she was formerly acquainted. Their premarital letters represent the most unmistakable evidence of romantic love of the educated men and women of the nineteenth century. On reading these letters, we may appreciate how intimate the pre-nuptial relationship between bride and groom had become in one section of the society and how changed was the manner in which they addressed each other. Pramath Chaudhuri and Indira Devi exchanged a total of forty letters in September 1898. But this kind of communion, familiarity, or exchange of letters prior to marriage was rare, even amongst the educated, in Bengali society at large. The actual relationship could develop between the husband and the wife only after marriage. It was during the latter half of the nineteenth century that the attempts on the part of some educated men to fashion a like-minded companion in one's own wife was most noticeable.[55]

Towards the close of the nineteenth century, we are introduced to an absolutely different conjugal relationship. Rabindranath taught his wife Mrinalini Devi to garner unwavering intellectual and spiritual strength in order to develop firm endurance. This is evident from the letters Rabindranath wrote to his wife. In 1892, he wrote in a letter to his wife, "If we traverse the easy path with firm strength under all circumstances then the improper conduct of the others need not cause any disquiet in us—perhaps just trying this much would enable our heart to be moulded thus." In the same year he writes in another letter to Mrinalini Devi that: "Don't nurse dissatisfaction, *choto bou*[56] no good comes of it." Six years later, in 1898, Rabindranath advised his wife to remain steadfast under all circumstances: "In the romance of a man and a woman in youth there is a heady intoxication but perhaps this you realize from your own experience—that it is in maturity amidst the call of see-sawing household existence that the truly steadfast, deep, controlled, silent play of man-woman's love is initiated—with the expansion of one's own family the external world recedes further and further—that is why there is a sense of solitude alongside the growth of the family and the two are entwined in the embrace of the close bonds of relationships ....May the two of us support each other's humanism, offer the private sanctuary to the heart wearied of household demands and help each other in spending our lives gracefully, till the very end."[57]

Within the familiar Bengali tradition where the wife had never been granted the dignity that she deserved, the letter mirrors a conjugal intimacy amidst the insignificant details of household life. It expresses above all the ideal of mutual dependence and partnership. This ideal is perhaps the greatest culmination of the changing attitudes of the last few decades. This was unimaginable in the traditional conjugal relationship in Bengal. This transformation takes shape very slowly and almost imperceptibly. Thus, when Nikhilesh in the novel *Ghare Baire* desires to bring Bimala out in the world and forge a relationship with her there, he represents the newly educated Bengali and his transformed attitude. The realisation that in order to enjoy a more intimate relationship with the wife, she needs to be in a freer environment and not confined is the result of this changed attitude. The two other sisters-in-law of Bimala never experienced this. They knew that the antahpur was their only horizon. Bimala's stepping out thus appeared grotesque in their eyes, as they were unfamiliar with the changing attitudes of the time. Bimala's sisters-in-law never enjoyed their husbands' company as she did, which added perhaps to the sense of deprivation in the life of the second sister-in-law. This would have been true of the majority of women of the nineteenth century. Not only Bimala's second sister-in-law but also the conservative society was largely cold in its reaction to this new way of thinking. The difference between those emancipated by the new ideas and the tradition-bound section is primarily that of education, taste, and thought process. Thus, despite being contemporaries, they often appear to be poles apart, and this ensuing conflict is the primary determining character of the nineteenth-century consciousness.

Notes

1. This article has been excerpted and translated from chapter three (*Dampatya Bhavana*) and chapter four (*Ghar-Grhyasthali*), Sambuddha Chakrabarti, "Andare Antare", *Stree*, Calcutta, 1995, by the editors of this volume. The author has written a new introduction and conclusion for this article.
2. Rabindranath Tagore, *Ghare Baire, Rabindra Upanyas Sangraha,* Calcutta, Viswabharati, 1997, 852.
3. Sarojini Devi, 'Paribare Shishushikshya', (The Education of the Child in the Family), *Antahpur, Jaistha,*1903, 33.
4. *Bankim Racanabali* (volume I), Calcutta, Sahitya Samsad Samaskaran, 1954, 291.
5. "Bangiya Hindu Samaj-Samaskar", *Bangamahila, Caitra,* 1875, 278.
6. "Paribarik Samaskar", *Bangamahila, Magh,* 1875, 235.
7. "Grihini", *Sadharani,* 23rd *Caitra,* 1879, 276.
8. *Bamabodhini Patrika, Bhadra,* 1884, 143.
9. *Sadharani,* 23rd *Caitra,* 1879, 276.
10. *Antahpur, Agrahayan,* 1902, 150.
11. *Bangamahila, Magh,* 1875, 235.
12. *Bangamahila, Magh,* 1875, 236.
13. *Antahpur, Agrahayan,* 1902, 150.
14. Satiprakash Sen, "Koner Bou", *Somprakash,* 15th *Baisakh,*1880, 15.
15. ibid.
16. "Sasurir Atyacar", *Paricarika, Agrahayan,* 1891, 179.
17. Jnanadanandini Devi's 'Smritikatha', Indira Devi Choudhurani, ed., *Puratani,* Kolkata, 1879 Sakabda, 21.
18. Harihar Sheth, *Gharer Katha* (Chandan Nagar 1924), 84–86. According to the date of publication, *Gharer Katha* is a twentieth-century composition, but this has been written in the author's old age and the nineteenth century has cast its shadow on the text time and again.
19. "Badhushashan", *Bamabodhini Patrika, Aswin,* 1887, 162.
20. *Garer Katha,* 89.
21. Sivnath Sastri, *Yugantar,* Kolkata, 1967, 145.
22. Sivnath Sastri, *Yugantar,* 147.
23. *Dena Paona* was written in 1891. It was published in the journal, *Hitbadi.* But as no file of this journal has hitherto been discovered, there is some doubt over this date.

24. Jnanadanandini Devi, 'Smritikatha', *Puratani*, 36.
25. *Paricarika, Jaistha-Asadh*, 1885, 34.
26. *Bharat-Mahila, Jaistha*, 1907, 39.
27. *Shadharani*, 23 *Caitra*, 1879, 277.
28. *Rasasundar Devir Atmakatha*, Nareshchandra Jana, Manu Jana, Kamal Kumar Sanyal, eds., volume I, Kolkata, 19.
29. *Kailashbasini Devir Atmakatha*, volume II Kolkata, 1982, 16–17.
30. Prafullamoyi Devi, 'Amader Katha', *Prabasi, Baishakh*, 1930, 113.
31. Prasannamoyi Devi, *Purba Katha*, 1917, Kolkata, 1982, 44.
32. *Antahpur, Agrahayan*, 1902, 150.
33. 'Paribarik Sukh', *Paricarika, Baisakh*, 1890, 149.
34. Banalata Devi, 'Ramanir Paribarik O Samaik Kartabya', *Antahpur, Baisakh*, 1903, 9.
35. *Atmakatha*, volume I, 37.
36. 'Bangamahila', *Bamabodhini Patrika, Baisakh*, 1874, 12.
37. 'Banganarider Abasthya' *Mahila, Kartik*, 1906, 88.
38. Chitra Dev, *Antapurer Atmakatha*, Kolkata, 1984, 86.
39. Debipada Bhattacharya, ed., *Reverend Lal Behari Dey O Chandramukhir Upakhyan*, Kolkata 1968, 5.
40. *Kalikal* refers to the Hindu mythical age of catastrophe.
41. Upendranath Bhattacharya, *Ajogya Parinay*, Kolkata, 1879, 34.
42. Dhirendranath Pal, *Strir Sahit Kathopakan*, volume I, Kolkata, no date of publication, 53.
43. *Paricharika, Asadh*, 1879, 84.
44. Tarakchandra Churamani, *Sapatni Natak*, Kolkata, 1857, 13.
45. Edward Storrow, *The Eastern Lily Gathered*, London, 1858, 42.
46. Indira Devi Chaudhurani, ed., *Puratani*, Kolkata, 1879, Sakabda, 27.
47. Girishchandra Sen, *Brahmamayi Carit*, Kolkata, 1869, 6.
48. Nareshchandra Jana, etc., ed., *Saradasundarir Atmakatha*, volume I, Kolkata, 1982, 11.
49. Jyotirmoyi Mukhopadhyaya, *Tattvabhushan Jivani*, Kolkata, 1959, 45.
50. *Puratani*, op cit. 33.
51. Satyendranath Tagore, *Amar Balyakatha O Amar Bombai Prabash*, Kolkata, 1915, 5.
52. *Rabindra Rachanabali*, volume I, Kolkata, birth centenary edition, 1961, 469–70.
53. *Rabindra Rachanabali*, volume I, Kolkata, birth centenary edition, 1961, 471.

54. Sudakhshina Sen, *Jivan Smriti,* Kolkata, 1932, 106–08.
55. Also to be noted are attempts by Prakashchandra Roy and Aghorekamini Devi who tried hard to curb their physical desire in order establish an example of "pure" conjugal love; through the austere, ascetic control of the sensual they wanted to experience the spiritual qualities of life.
56. The term literally means "the younger wife"; here the appellation refers to Mrinalini's status as the wife of the youngest son, Rabindranath Tagore, within the extended family. *Bhai Chotobou: Strike Lekha Rabindranather Chithi*, Purva, Kolkata, 2003, 22.
57. *Bhai Chotobou : Strike Lekha Rabindranather Chithi*, Purva, Kolkata, 2003, 29.

4

Teaching the Wife: Miss Gilby, the English Women, and the Antahpur

SHAMPA ROY

> Jane, you are docile, diligent, disinterested, faithful, constant and courageous; very gentle and very heroic. As a conductress of Indian schools and as a helper amongst Indian women, your assistance to me will be invaluable (*Jane Eyre* 1847).

> And it came to Miss Crane then that the only excuse she or anyone of her kind had to be there, sitting on the chair, the object of the awe of the uninstructed women, was if they sat there conscious of a duty to promote the cause of human dignity and interest (*The Jewel in the Crown* 1966).

> When my husband brought in Miss Gilby to teach me and be my companion, he stuck to his resolve in spite of the poison secreted by all the wagging tongues at home and outside (*The Home and The World* 1916).

The juxtaposition of the reference to Miss Gilby with St John's earnest exhortation to Jane Eyre to go to India to teach Indian women and the sombre description of Miss Crane's decision to become a teacher in India helps locate Bimala's English teacher in the tradition of the genteel English spinster for whom colonial India had opened up "opportunities" in the form of teaching natives, especially native women. The image that grew and gathered strength over the years of such English women was that of fiercely dedicated, kindly women detached from the oppressive workings of Imperial politics, silently carrying on with their noble reformatory work in adverse circumstances.[1] So powerful is the image that rarely has the actual nature of what they taught the native women been considered worthy of scrutiny. The emancipatory and beneficial impact of their teaching was simply taken for granted. In *The Home and The World,* even though Miss Gilby is a peripheral figure, the implications of her presence in Nikhilesh's household as a teacher and companion to his wife are worth examining, given the way the situation is instrumentalised for consolidating his credentials as a liberal husband and an enlightened individual.[2]

When an older and "maturer" Bimala recounts the initial years of conjugality with her modern, Western-educated husband, one of the first things she remembers ruefully is his painstaking efforts to recast her. With some irony and implied criticism of her earlier naivete, she also recalls her own failure to appreciate his efforts whole-heartedly.[3] Not only is Nikhilesh's exceptional liberality and emancipated masculinity established through the contrast with his dead brother—a debauched and abusive husband—it is reaffirmed through his various measures to steer Bimala firmly away from her traditional notions of good wifehood, domestic drudgery, and the petty competitiveness of the antahpur towards his project of reformed conjugality.

> My husband used to say, that man and wife are equal in love because of their equal claim on each other... "I would have you come into the heart of the outer world and meet reality. Merely going on with your household duties, living all your life in the world of household conventions and the drudgery of household tasks,—you were not made for that! If we meet and recognise each other in the real world, only then will our love be true."(18)

One such measure is the bringing in of Miss Gilby as her teacher and companion. The reader is not told exactly how Miss Gilby contributes to the project of emancipating Bimala from her cloistered, drudgery-filled world and conservative ideas of wifehood and urging her towards a more equal conjugality. Implicit in the reference to Miss Gilby seems to be the assumption that an English woman's influence and teaching are invariably emancipatory and that therefore the husband who makes them available to his wife is definitionally enlightened and progressive. Subsequently, when Miss Gilby is humiliated and attacked by some boys in the name of swadeshi, she is seen as the innocent victim of the kind of gratuitous and excessive anti-colonial violence that Nikhilesh and the text are so critical of. In fact, through his grave condemnation of such activities—a response that Nikhilesh stresses through his gesture of accompanying Miss Gilby to the railway station—he is reinstated as the figure of quiet courage, rationality, and tolerance. Also, his plaintive appeal to Bimala: "Can you not get over the barrier of her name after such a long acquaintance? Can not you realise that she loves you?" (25) is not only meant to admonish her for being racist and parochial, but it also stresses the rational need to see Miss Gilby's presence as one made possible by "love" and not by the Empire (reinforced wonderfully in the film by the frail and gentle-looking Kendall).

Despite Nikhilesh's reproachful statement, however, a critical examining of the unquestioned assumptions surrounding Miss Gilby—that English women like her invariably helped emancipate women like Bimala from their tradition-bound lives or that their reformatory concern could be separated from Imperial politics—does not have to be seen as being associated with the condoning of violence against her. The viewing of Miss Gilby through a "mist of abstractions", for which Nikhilesh berates his wife, might be better redressed not by the diffuse ideal of universal love that he suggests, but through a locating of the English female teacher in colonial Indian history.[4] Such positioning can lead not only to a better understanding of the role of genteel English spinsters like Miss Gilby in India but also to an uncovering of some of the unproblematised assumptions that help establish Nikhilesh's status as a liberal and progressive bhadralok.

English women's reformatory concern for their "Indian sisters" dovetailed with the rise of the single, "redundant" women of England looking for greater work opportunities and also with the emergence of middle-class feminists looking for more powerful ways of self-authorisation.[5] As British middle-class women struggled with questions of their own social and legal emancipation, they began to look increasingly upon the issue of Indian women's reform as a site that offered them with opportunities for empowering work outside the domestic space, and this was the kind of work for which they felt they were specially equipped. With travel to India becoming much easier following the opening of the Suez Canal, single women like Mary Carpenter and Annette Beveridge—predecessors of Miss Gilby—embarked on journeys to India with the intention of acquiring experiential knowledge about the "condition" of Indian women and exploring the possibilities of English women like themselves helping in their reform.

The pitiful "condition" of Indian women had functioned as a shorthand for the degraded state of India in a number of colonial writings since the eighteenth century, including James Mill's *History of British India* (1840), a definitive text on Indian history for many contemporary English officials including Macaulay. The need to rescue Indian women and ameliorate their suffering had been projected by the East India Company officials as a moral responsibility that helped legitimise the Empire. Till the 1860s, however, English women who came to India saw their roles as confined to observing scenes and documenting them. Even though they visited *zenanas* and bemoaned the condition of Indian women in them, in their travel writings, they made it quite clear that the actual reform work was to be left to the masculine discretion and enterprise of the colonial rulers. It was from the 1860s with the emergence of the bourgeois feminist movement in England that reform of Indian women was seen by English women as appropriate feminine work and was persistently written about in those terms.[6]

From the 1860s, thus began a century of what Antoinette Burton calls "Imperial feminism", whereby English feminists' concern for their Indian sisters and their urging English women to work for their cause became a regular feature of the feminist agenda. Such concern, though sincere, paid no attention to the Indian women's own voices and was based on the reading of Indian women as being invariably incapable of resisting oppressive practices on their own and therefore requiring reformatory gestures from their Western sisters.[7] Furthermore, even as these English women trangressed traditional norms of feminine behaviour themselves in seeking to do work outside the domestic space, their reform agenda for Indian women was based on the most rigid and oppressive Victorian notions of proper middle-class femininity.

Mary Carpenter's *Six Months in India*, a travel account published in 1868 that records her own experiences with female reform in India and also contains elaborate proposals for educating the wives of the Bengali bhadralok, is fraught with such contradictions. Carpenter's travelogue, on its publication in 1868, was hailed by contemporary English feminists as evidence of the serious work that women were capable of doing in the colonies, and Carpenter, despite her ambivalent response to the feminist movement, was appropriated as a role model by contemporary feminist activists.[8] Carpenter's record of her own experiences with female reform in India had two important consequences for the feminist movement in Britain. It gave their reformist enthusiasm a new and more challenging subject—the Indian woman—and it expanded the boundaries of the terrain of feminine work. Carpenter's impassioned writing about "the increasing need for women's work in India" and her exhortation to fellow English women to "arise and devote themselves to the glorious and blessed work of raising their Indian sisters to fill that place in society for which the Creator has destined them" gave a powerful and much-needed impetus to this project, and henceforth most feminist writings talked of the importance of English women's work on behalf of their "Indian sisters" (I, 79). Her *Six Months in India* is thus worth examining in order to see how, despite her conviction articulated in 1856 that her "work is to be done not by attempting for myself any public action for which my woman's nature quite unfits me", she scripts an authoritative identity capable of effectually fulfilling public roles on the site of Indian women's reform.[9] The analysis also necessarily entails looking at the extent to which her reform agenda, which responds sympathetically to the anxious desire of the English-educated local patriarchy for suitable companions, actually sought to transform the lives of the Bengali bhadramahila.

Carpenter's "knowledge" of India and of the "problem" of Indian women was based on her encounters with some Bengali reformers who had come to Britain and who, like most middle-class Bengali reformers of the mid- to late nineteenth century, were very concerned about the "condition" of Bengali middle-class women. In the first chapter of *Six Months in India*, Carpenter recalls, in language redolent of Victorian cultural presumptions about a lurid and exotic East, that it was the "graphic and fearful ...picture of the condition of Hindoo women" apprehended from a public lecture given by a Brahmin bhadralok in England that inspired her to "form the resolve to do something to ameliorate their condition." Thus, for Carpenter, Indian women were not only constituted as a "problem" by the English-educated Bengali men before she even got to India, but her "knowledge" about their status and condition was also mediated through these men who, according to Carpenter, came to Britain "to become acquainted with English men and women in their public and private work... and thus to qualify themselves on their return to India to transplant there what they have found deserving of imitation amongst us."[10]

The project of recasting and educating Bengali middle-class women was indeed shaped by the Western-educated bhadralok's desire to enjoy the pleasures of *dampatya* with a "fit" companion as well as to transform the Bengali home along the ideals of middle-class Victorian domesticity. The reforming of domestic arrangements was also perceived as being tied up with the revivification of the nation. Since this critical task could not take place without making women aware of the importance of such changes, the question of the Hindu/Brahmo Bengali women's educational reform began to occupy centre stage in many public discussions and debates from the 1850s. Bhadralok reformers were, of course, frequently haunted by the spectre of *strishiksha* leading to denationalised and defeminised women. They continued to eulogise such mystified patriarchal ideals of female chastity and decorous behaviour as *lajja* (shame), *sheelata* (propriety), *satitwa* (chastity), and *shobhanata* (sobriety) and to insist on the inseparability of these values from the identity of the reformed Hindu woman.[11] But they were equally anxious to create a "new woman", who would be an enlightened and able manager of the reconstructed private space. This reformed new woman was thus going to be untrammelled by the demands and restrictions that were perceived as being endemic to joint-familial arrangements, but only to become more fully available to the claims and demands of husband and children within the nucleated domestic space. Carpenter's travelogue, despite being full of concern for Indian women, sympathises with and privileges the needs and anxieties of the patriarchal bhadralok, and her suggested educative programme for Bengali women colludes with the bhadralok's desire to have wives who would be devoted to domestic duties, to wifehood, and motherhood within the nucleated space.

Even though Bengali bhadramahilas themselves had not begun to participate in these debates in any considerable way at the time Carpenter visited India, they were not entirely a silent constituency either. In 1866, for instance, Brahmo women had formed an association for genteel women called Brahmika Samaj. Writings by bhadramahilas had begun to appear in some periodicals, and there are some that contain sharp critiques of patriarchal practices and a demand for change.[12]

From the late 1860s onwards, in fact, a few bhadramahilas formed women's organisations some of which included in their aims a refusal to depend on men and a resistance to any imposition of Western values. Despite having met some of the members of the recently established Brahmika Samaj, Carpenter, in her writing, does not individualise Indian women nor grant them subjectivity.

In *Six Months in India*, for instance, sympathetic concern for the condition of Indian women is frequently based on easy orientalist equations between Hinduism/vice/unfitness for proper feminine roles. Carpenter collapses Indian/Hindu/Bengali women into a single, reductive category and represents them as being superstition-ridden, enclosed in unhygienic, "sunless, airless" spaces and "utterly ignorant of all that should exalt her nature".[13] Zenana-cloistered and ignorant, they are, however, seen as being capable of exercising a pernicious influence on the Western-educated men in the families, who seem therefore to be as much in need of rescue as their female relatives. Carpenter, in fact, persistently identifies the native gentlemen as pitiable figures trapped in households where unenlightened women exercise a "remarkable sway" over them (76). "None," she bemoans, "can be more alive to the evils of woman's present position than enlightened Hindoos themselves, who perceive in it, not only the loss of that high domestic happiness which they have learnt to aspire to as their own natures have become more elevated by education, but also the grand barrier to the great improvement of their race, and their own emancipation from the thralldom of superstition" (75). She describes, for instance, the travails of a young educated Bengali college student in great detail:

> Whether we read the description given by the collegian of the degrading manner in which the young Bengali, whose mind has been imbued with the highest and the purest sentiments of English Literature, is compelled by his female relatives to pay his morning homage before a senseless image... or whether we listen with astonishment to a native judge who publicly confesses that he had been compelled by the ladies of the household to do what he knows to be wrong... exclaiming helplessly, "Some men may boast that they have moral courage, I have not; who can curb a woman?"—every view of the subject directs us to the same point; all acknowledge that the present condition of woman and her utter ignorance of everything that should exalt her nature, is the greatest barrier to the elevation of the natives (76).

What is quite apparent from such a description is that the reform project for Indian women seeks to redress the hapless misery of the enlightened bhadralok and their tragic entrapment in debilitating domestic arrangements in which ignorant women act as petty tyrants. The repeated prioritising of the bhadralok's perspective and of the need to alleviate their misery at having uneducated wives obliterates possible questions about why women's emancipation must necessarily be linked to the goals of domestic happiness and companionship. Furthermore, the reform project, it is made quite clear, is to be a collaborative project between emancipated English women and the beleaguered bhadralok, and Bengali women are to be its silently grateful recipients:

> I have thus been enabled to devise a scheme which...will prove a great blessing to the country and meet the wants of the enlightened native population by enabling them to obtain the help of educated English women in the elevation of their wives and daughters (216).

The deployment of Bengali women in this manner—as figures of misguided, unenlightened power—also confirms the cultural hierarchies on which Carpenter bases her own assumption of a self-consolidating pedagogic role. Indian women are inferior cultural counterfoils to emancipated English women like herself, who have enjoyed the benefits of a "liberal" education in England where women are regarded as "fellow-workers and helpers of men":

> All of you are aware that in England women hold a very different position from that which they occupy in India. In England they are regarded as fellow-workers with and helpers of men. By giving them a liberal education, it is not intended that they should take the place of the other sex but that they should be better qualified than they would otherwise be (222).

What she seems to be suggesting here is that one of the obvious markers of England's well-deserved position of cultural superiority is the liberty that it accords to its women—a suggestion that erases the ongoing struggle by feminists in England for greater rights and liberties. Besides, Carpenter approvingly refers to the English education that consolidates gender hierarchies as "liberal". Such a description does not explain why she then needs to transgress the gender roles prescribed by this "liberal" education in seeking the sense of empowerment and fulfilment that she herself talks of as having achieved by performing stridently public roles.

Sliding over such contradictions between her pronouncements about appropriate education for women and her own transgressions of the gender roles that were intrinsic to such education, she goes on to premise her educational reform programme for Indian women on the most conservative and rigid notions of proper Victorian bourgeois femininity—devotion to domestic duties, to wifehood, and to motherhood within the nucleated family. This programme while offering some kind of a break from the past for the Bengali wives and daughters, seems to be preparing them ultimately for reconstituted patriarchal relations within the nucleated familial space and thus, in the final analysis, colludes with the needs and desires of the bhadralok.

The main aim of female education, Carpenter frequently assures her audience in the public speeches that she quotes in her text, is to "enable them to become better wives, better mothers and thus more useful members of society. By women, the infant minds of both sexes are trained..." (223). At another point she pathologises Indian women in terms of their ineffective mothering:

> Extreme ignorance and the vices connected with idolatory, render women in India very unfit to perform the duty nature intended for her—the care of children; for even if she can take proper care of their little bodies (which is doubtful) she infuses into their opening minds a degree of deception and willfulness which years may not be able to eradicate (80).

Since women's education must focus on dispensing skills aimed at making them better mothers or mothers-to-be, Carpenter's repeatedly stated demand for female teachers is also based on the inadequacy of male teachers in disseminating these uniquely feminine qualities to their female students. Thus, according to her, they require

> proper influence in the manners and character which a female teacher can give. The training to habits of neatness and order, instruction in needlework which are so essential in a woman, in whatever position in life she may be placed are necessarily neglected (if taught by a male teacher)....(143)

In this she sounds no different from the ponderous voices that abound in the didactic literature produced in England since the early nineteenth century, which talk about the importance of teaching women feminine skills and accomplishments that would make them modest, efficient and contented helpmeets to their husbands.[14] Furthermore, she deploys the word "proper" not only to naturalise certain kinds of spaces, roles, and work as uniquely feminine but also to assign normative status to values linked to the lives of leisured domesticity available to upper-class Victorian women. She says, for instance, about working-class women that she has seen in India that:

> There has been as yet no organised attempt made to educate the girls of the inferior castes ...a great gulf actually exists between those who are secluded in the zenana and those who are rather the drudges and slaves of the other sex rather than their helpmates. The sight of women employed as ordinary labourers—as porters toiling under heavy burdens—is most repulsive. The features which nature intended to be soft and refined, are worn with hardship and the degrading employments they are compelled to undertake seems to destroy the sense of feminine propriety. Thus compelled to do the work of men, they are debarred from employments regarded by us as *properly belonging to women* (emphasis mine) (80–81).

The working-class women's access to the work space available to their husbands is seen as inevitably reducing them to unattractive, even non-feminine, "drudges ...not helpmates", for it is incapable of nurturing that precious feminine elegance which alone is seen as making a woman complete.[15] At another point she describes with genteel horror such women gathered at the *ghat* to "perform their ablution and for various household purposes, such as drawing water and washing clothes" as being "wholly devoid of any feeling akin to delicacy". In India she goes on to assert, "the voices and manner of the lower classes of women appeared to me more harsh and coarse than those of the men....It would seem as if the great seclusion of the women of the higher classes withdraws the refining influence of their sex from society...those who are not so shielded are thus left in the rude position of barbaric life" (85)[16]. While elsewhere in *Six Months in India* Carpenter talks of the "sunless, airless" existence of the zenana women as leading to their degraded existence, here by some curious twist of logic, it is the secluded lives of such women that leads to their being shielded from coarseness. On the other hand, leading their lives outside the zenanas seems to make the working-class women devoid of that ineffable quality of "delicacy"—a hypostatised feminine virtue that resonates with upper-class Victorian notions of privatised, chaste, and leisured lives. Quite obviously then, the appeal of her solemn reform project for Indian wives and mothers as far as the emergent bhadralok was concerned also lay in its goal of socialising those women into a kind of femininity that was significantly tied up with acquiring the appropriate and distinguishing markers of genteel existence.

By the late Victorian period, even as a number of English women became actively involved in the suffragette movement in metropolitan England and demanded political enfranchisement for themselves, they continued to write about their unfortunate sisters of the Empire as voiceless, helpless, ignorant women who awaited their attention and intervention in order to become good wives and mothers. This image of the "Indian woman" exercised a general ideological force and even after Rukhmabai, Kadambini Ganguli, and others entered the medical profession and Pandita Ramabai articulated a forceful critique of contemporary patriarchy, English women's certainties about the readymade clientele of the zenanas and their requirements never made them redefine the kind of educative programme formulated by Carpenter in her writings which was based on the rigid separation of spheres.

Nikhilesh's complicity in such a limited project of reform becomes evident from the fact that while he does not want his wife to worship his feet, he does desire a companion who would express her devotion to him by appreciating his costly gifts, his courtship rituals, and his swadeshi efforts. While he talks to Bimala of the importance of their meeting and recognising each other in the real world, "the real world" for Bimala never becomes anything more than the drawing room, and the extent of her freedom, not more than being able to step out of the antahpur and play gracious hostess to Nikhilesh's friends. Even when he tempts her with the offer of moving to Calcutta, "leaving behind the sister-in-law, the consolation of ruling over the household, and giving their life at the same time, more room to branch out", it is not very clear as to how he conceptualises such greater branching out for Bimala. It is true that he expects the educated Bimala to distance herself from the petty competitiveness and jealousies of the zenana, but it is equally true that there is no role he can conceptualise for her beyond that of an elegant recipient of his romantic gestures.[17] He sulks bitterly therefore at having his "worship" spurned and at Bimala's choice of participation in the Swadeshi Andolan in its place:

> My wife!—Have I not cherished in this little world all that is purest and sweetest in my life, never for a moment letting it down from my bosom to the dust? What incense of worship, what music of passion, what flowers of my spring and of my autumn, have I not offered up at its shrine? If like a toy paper boat she be swept along into the muddy waters of the gutter…(78)

The harsh, judgmental language used for Bimala's choice of something other than what he had in mind for her is of course justified in the text by the collapsing of this alternative with a necessary submission to Sandip's insidious influence. Nikhilesh's autocritique never extends to the point of seeing that despite his emancipatory project, Bimala might want something beyond the ideal of marital felicity. Her desire is briefly articulated in the text, for instance, in the section where she envisions the future of womanhood in terms of freedom from the conventions of domestic and maternal roles, and in language that seems to suggest a powerful opposition to the putative notions of proper femininity embedded in the writings of women like Carpenter:

> In that future I saw my country, a woman like myself, standing expectant. She has been drawn forth from her home corner by the call of some Unknown. She has had no time to pause, or ponder, or to light herself a torch, as she rushes forward into the darkness ahead. I know well how her soul responds to the distant flute-strains which call her; how her breast rises and falls; how she feels when she nears it; nay it is already hers, so that it matters not even if she ran blindfold. *She is no mother. There is no call to her of children in their hunger, no home to be lighted of an evening, no household work to be done.* No, she hies to her tryst, for this is the land of the Vaishnava poets. *She has left home, forgotten domestic duties; she has nothing but an unfathomable yearning which hurries her on*—by what road, to which goal, she recks not. I also am possessed of just such a yearning. I likewise have lost my way. Both the end and the means have become equally shadowy to me (120, emphasis mine).

While there is an element of hyperbole in her vision, the references to a woman's yearning for a life outside of conjugality and motherhood, strip the prevalent ideals of femininity (even reformed femininity) of their obfuscatory rhetoric. However, this countervailing possibility remains largely unexplored in the text, and a genuine showdown between the claims of participation in swadeshi, on the one hand, and marriage, on the other, is averted by practically reducing swadeshi to the unprincipled villainy of Sandip. Nothing remains then, it seems, but for Bimala to return, chastened and contrite, to Nikhilesh and to seeking of penance through the conservative ideals of wifely devotion and voluntary obedience. The conclusion then reaffirms the ideal of greater fitness for ameliorated conjugal relations as the end of the reform project for women with which the text had begun—an ideal that the contemporary bhadralok had forcefully argued for and, with the aid of English women like Miss Gilby, had made the basis of the agenda for their wives' emancipation.

Notes

1. Even though Jane Eyre does not actually go to India to teach native women, there is undoubtedly a great deal of admiration in the text for women who do make the choice to be "grilled alive in Calcutta". Miss Crane in Paul Scott's novel is a doughty and earnest teacher (the kind that Jane would have become had she taken the other road) in a school for Indian girls whose devotion to duty as well as liberal ideals are indicated through her determined cycling through crowded bazaars and bad roads to reach the village school regardless of weather and her frequent questioning of the legitimacy of the British rule. Attacked like Miss Gilby by some Indian rowdies during the Quit India Movement, she refuses to identify the men when asked by the police, and, subsequently, in an act of protest against the embittered inter-racial relations that had led to the assault, decides to commit a heroic sati.
2. The presence of Miss Gilby, for instance, is seen as being important enough to merit inclusion in Ray's film (with an actress of no less than Jennifer Kendall's stature playing the part)—a film that otherwise takes several liberties with the written text.
3. Of the three accounts that constitute the narrative, it is only Bimala's that reports the events as if they happened in the past. Consequently, Bimala's accounts are never a simple recounting of the past. For there is always an accompanying sense of the older Bimala's "maturer" and wistful perspective on what happened back then. As a result of this strategic device, her critical responses or resistance to Nikhilesh's decisions are put in ironic perspective, and seen as childish petulance or partial understanding of things. What this means is that the truth and greatness of Nikhilesh are never really questioned for the *telos* of Bimala's *bildungsroman* seems to have been the unquestioned acceptance of her husband's views.
4. "I cannot," my husband said, "look upon Miss Gilby through a mist of abstractions, just because she is English." *The Home and The World,* trans. Surendranath Tagore, New Delhi, Macmillan, reprint 1999, 25.
5. The word "redundant" was used by W. R. Greg, a liberal manufacturer, to describe single women in an essay that addresses the "problem" of their enormous numbers in Britain. Titled, "Why are Women Redundant?", the essay talks about "an enormous and increasing number of single women in the nation, a number quite disproportionate

and abnormal...most numerous in the middle and upper classes...who have to earn their own living, instead of spending and husbanding the earnings of men." See W. R. Greg, "Why are Women Redundant?" *National Review,* 14, 1862, 436, qtd. in Mary Poovey, *Uneven Developments: Ideological Work of Gender in Mid-Victorian England,* Chicago, Univ. of Chicago Press, 1988, 1.

6. Philanthropic work, even before feminists appropriated it for their activist agenda, had been seen as fit occupation for genteel single women. Often represented as a form of vicarious mothering whereby these "superfluous" women could gratify their powers "healthily, innocently, usefully", it was seen as transforming these unattached, potentially disruptive women into disciplined subjects. When feminists appropriated reform for emancipatory purposes, they stressed its importance as serious and socially useful work and used it to challenge the Victorian ideology of "separate spheres".
7. Antoinette Burton, "States of Injury: Josephine Butler on Slavery, Citizenship and the Boer War," *Social Politics* 5 no. 3, 1998, 338. One does not doubt the beneficent intent of these women, but, as pointed out by James Buzzard, "sincere beneficent intentions can nevertheless be ideologically produced or encouraged." See James Buzzard, "Victorian Women and the Implications of Empire," *Victorian Studies* 36 no. 4 (Summer), 1993, 448.
8. At the time that Carpenter embarked on the project of Indian female reform and wrote about the opportunities available to middle-class English women, the middle-class Victorian women's movement had grown from what it had initially started out—as a committee demanding greater rights for married women—to one that was beginning to campaign for the vote. In the early 1860s, Barbara Bodichon's committee for like-minded women, which had petitioned for married women's property rights, purchased a building where they initiated a number of ventures designed to promote the winning of women's rights. They published the *English Women's Journal,* convinced college authorities to allow women students to attend classes, and by 1865, they had organised the Women's Suffrage Committee.
9. J. E. Carpenter, *The Life and Work of Mary Carpenter,* London, Macmillan, 1879, 165. Carpenter had in fact been a young girl when Rammohun Roy had travelled to England and had befriended her father, but even then she had been deeply impressed with his personality. She had therefore known about Indian women's problems

for a very long time. However, it was not until 1860, when worn out with over-work and depressed by her father's death, she felt a strong wish for a complete change "if I am to shake off mournful remembrances", that she began to think of India as "a new field... where (my) natural powers will have free scope". See Carpenter 309, 299.

10. Mary Carpenter, *The Last Days in England of the Rajah Rammohun Roy,* Calcutta, Riddhi, 1866, qtd. in Burton, 554.
11. They were equally eager to segregate the bhadra femininity from that of lower-class/lower-caste women. See Sumanta Banerjee, "Marginalisation of Women's Popular Culture in Nineteenth Century Bengal" in Sangari and Vaid, 127–79.
12. Madhumati Ganguli, for instance, writes in the *Bamabodhini Patrika* in 1864, "Dear Bengali sisters! We have been created by the same God who created men. He has given men and women the same organs, feelings, and faculties of mind. Men are acquiring learning and wisdom and are meeting with his blessings... Why should we be deprived? God certainly does not wish that only men enjoy the pleasure of learning and women the agony of ignorance. On the contrary, He has given men the same physical and mental abilities so that both can enjoy endless happiness by acquiring the wealth of learning." See Madhumati Ganguli, "Bamaganer Rachana," (The Writings of Women) *Bamabodhini Patrika* (Oct.–Nov.) 1864, 229, qtd. in Ghulam Murshid, *The Reluctant Debutante: The Response of Bengali Women to Modernisation 1849–1905,* Rajshahi, Rajshahi UP, 1983, 53. The *Bamabodhini Patrika* (Journal for the Enlightenment of Women) was started by Umeshchandra Dutt in 1862 as a journal for advocating strishiksha (female education) and creating a space for women to write about their own lives and experiences. In other similar contributions to the journal, one woman writes, "Why have men kept us in such a low state? Are we not the children of the Great Father? How much longer do we stay chained to our homes?" Another complains bitterly, "We women live lives that are no better than those of animals." See Soudamini Debi, *Bamabodhini Patrika* (1865) and Kamini Debi, *Bamabodhini Patrika* (1865), qtd. in Bharati Ray, *Sekaaler Narishiksha*: *Bamabodhini Patrika,* 1862–1919 (Female Education in Those Times), Calcutta, 1996, 27, 45.
13. Mary Carpenter, *Six Months in India,* London, Longmans Green, 1868, 76. Ironically enough, while some of the Bengali women,

whom Carpenter had met, wrote about the importance of the kind of interaction with men that such meetings organised to felicitate Carpenter had made possible, male reformers like Keshub Chandra Sen frowned severely upon these mixed gatherings.

14. The Victorian ideal of female education was based on the assumption that women, rather than being called upon to "disentangle the knotty questions of the political economist", would be responsible for organising the household, bringing up the children, and providing a haven of companionship, tranquility and moral purity to men seeking solace from the turbulent world outside. "Home is clearly woman's intended place; and the duties which belong to Home are Women's province. It is in the sweet sanctities of domestic life that women should be taught to recognise her sphere of most appropriate service." John W. Burgon, *To Educate Young Women like Young Men—A Thing Inexpedient and Immodest* (1884), qtd in Joan N. Burstyn, *Victorian Education and the Ideal of Womanhood*, London, Croom Helm, 1980, 32. The syllabus framed for Bengali female students followed this model quite closely. The emphasis of the syllabus was clearly on literature, music, art, embroidery, and hygiene. The topics, for instance, of a local essay-writing competition organised by the *Noakhali Strishiksha Sammelani* (The Noakhali Association for Women's Education) in 1912, indicate the kind of skills and qualities they were expected to be trained in. The topics were "The Art of Cooking and Serving", "Minor Diseases and their Prevention" and "Devotion towards Husbands" (trans. mine). See Binoybhushan Roy, *Antahpure Strishiksha: A Short History of Women's Education in Bengal*, Kolkata, Naya Udyog, 1998.
15. Such an educative programme for the bhadramahila based on the most rigid norms of Victorian femininity, by sharpening the class divisions between contemporary Bengali women, closed off spaces that were earlier available to the women of the upper-classes for greater interactive experiences with women of other classes and castes. As pointed out by Sumanta Banerjee, before the spread of this kind of education in bhadralok homes, a vast multitude of working women had access to the antahpurs. These women brought along with them songs and dances composed in the dialect and idioms of popular cultural forms, some of which contained sharp critiques of patriarchal practices or bawdy expressions of female sexuality. By expunging these elements from the antahpurs, the education that Carpenter promoted so keenly as a liberating force

for Indian wives and mothers, placed them more firmly under the surveillance of the patriarchal bhadralok. See Sumanta Banerjee, "Women's Popular Culture in Nineteenth Century Bengal" in Sangari and Vaid, 130–32.

16. In *Jane Eyre,* even though Jane does not finally go to India to teach Indian women, as an instructress at the village school where she teaches for a brief while, she derisively describes the young girls as being uniformly ("all alike") "hopelessly dull with faculties quite torpid" and as "heavy-looking, gaping rustics". As a way of "elevating" them she teaches them "grammar, geography and the finer kinds of needlework" and the rebellious and passionate Jane also takes great pleasure in watching them become "obliging and amiable" with "quiet and orderly manners" (*Jane Eyre,* Penguin Books, 362).
17. It is also worth noting that the antahpur woman like the widowed Mejorani is represented in ways that are reminiscent of Carpenter's writing about them as being pernicious, superstition-ridden, and ignorant. While Nikhilesh reminds Bimala that women like Mejorani deserve her compassion, not censure, his own reform efforts remain exclusively and obsessively focussed on his wife, thus consolidating the marginalised status of women like the Mejorani. Besides indicating the contradiction in Nikhilesh's own reform efforts, this also points to the inadequacy of the reform gestures of women like Carpenter, who conceptualised emancipated feminine roles exclusively in terms companionate conjugality and enlightened maternity.

5

Goddesses, Women, and the Clutch of Metaphors in *Ghare Baire*

SASWATI SENGUPTA

> Are we only Lakshmi, it is we who are Bharati.[1]

This statement uttered by Bimala, brings together attributes of two goddesses, Lakshmi and Bharati. In popular Bengali Hindu imagination, Lakshmi is the beloved consort of Vishnu and the guardian angel of conjugal bliss.[2] She represents feminine beauty and also presides over familial and material well-being. Bharati is the nascent Indian nation, represented as a woman and deified as a goddess. She is a new member of the pantheon. One of the earliest references to feminised Bharat as the mother in Bengali literature is by Iswar Gupta (1812–59), the editor of the Bengali newspaper, *Sambad Prabhakar*. Bankimchandra Chattopadhyay's

(1838–94) hymn "Bande Mataram", first published in *Bangadarsan* in 1875 and later incorporated in the cultic novel *Anandamath* (1882), helped popularise this feminine figuration of the motherland. Abanindranath Tagore (1871–1951) also iconised, in 1904–05, the abstract ideal of nationalism in his painting of the country as a Mother carrying the promise of food, clothing, learning, and spiritual salvation. The painting was enlarged and used for a brief period in the swadeshi fund-raising processions of 1905–06 to the strains of Rabindranath Tagore's patriotic lyrics.[3] The politics of the colonised imbued Bharati, the nation as mother, with *shakti*, which is a conceptual focalisation of female strength as suggested by the different mother-goddess epiphanies of the Hindu pantheon.[4] The invocation of the worship of Shakti as an attribute of Bharati proliferated in the discourse of the colonised nation in nineteenth-century Bengal. The feminised nation straddled the mortal and the immortal realms through the juxtapositioning of the divine goddess and the familial mother. As the self-acknowledged peddler and exploiter of ideas, Sandip, admits in *Ghare Baire*, "There is an evolution of the gods too; the deities created by the ancestors must be changed according to the needs of the inheritors or else he will become an atheist" (165).

Are we only Lakshmi, it is we who are Bharati.

Metaphors are an indispensable basis of language and thought. Deployed to aid conceptualisation, metaphors negotiate meanings and structure judgment ideologically. Lakshmi is the sanctioned ideal of femininity, forever the happy wife. Metaphorised, she signals the approved and socially constructed domesticated woman. Bharati is a newer goddess. She hints a new role for women in a new public sphere—the nation. The deployment of the metaphor of goddesses in *Ghare Baire*, written by a Brahmo Tagore, is of critical importance, as the fiction of Bimala explores the complexities attendant upon an upper-caste Hindu woman's stepping out of the traditionally prescribed domestic realm at a moment in history when the nascent notion of nation was being debated and acted upon by the men of her society. Lakshmi and Bharati—together they construct the horizon of female expectation in Bimala's statement. The connecting "only" prevents a rupture between tradition and modernity and yet suggests the inadequacy of the traditional icon. Does Lakshmi ground the possibilities of Bharati? Can Bharati escape the clutch of the "true" forms of femininity of the Hindu tradition?

Are we only Lakshmi, it is we who are Bharati.

Bimala's assertive statement may be taken as an epiphanic moment of female self-construction. The chosen genre of autobiographical narration, *atmakathas*, and that too in colloquial diction, may augment the ideology of the discovery of the self through experience. But the utterance is not free floating. It is a statement made in a certain context within a fictional rendering of a charged moment in Bengal's history. Moreover, the imagined landscape of *Ghare Baire*, the context of Bimala's utterance, is constructed by not one but three voices: two male and one female. The plural voices emanating from the three atmakathas critique each other. The shifting perspectives refuse a simple or straight-forward meaning; monologic truth is thus deconstructed. Bimala's statement, a cryptic cultural code, derives meaning not in isolation but through other voices as well as the telos of the plot and the denouement of the novel.

"(My cousin sister Munu) has made a heaven of her impoverished home by the nectar of her heart. Today my entire being is crying out to just taste the food cooked by this Lakshmi... " (34). Thus speaks Nikhilesh, M.A. (Calcutta University), the modern liberal bhadralok of Bengal at the turn of the twentieth century. Nikhilesh desires here a manifested sight of Lakshmi in the avatar of his cousin sister Munu, who is a "good" wife to a poor man who, under the influence of alcohol, beats her regularly. In the meanwhile, Nikhilesh wishes his wife to dress in the "chemises, colourful jackets and petticoats"(10) bought from "English shops" (15), appoints an English teacher for her (20), gets her a pair of slippers through his Muslim friend from Lucknow (88), and prefers his wife's hair to be done up in an English bun (102). He is embarrassed to be "adored" by his wife (76), seeking instead an "equal relationship" (8). Nikhilesh is not immersed in alcohol and *nautch* girls which are his traditional patrimony. His is the enlightened mind that supports the right to female self-construction: "She is my wife and so she is mine alone! ...Is that an argument? Is that a truth? Can an entire being be wrapped up and locked within that word?" (62). Yet at the hour of his test as a liberal supporter of gender reforms, when his wife Bimala does step out of the private gendered quarters and is at the threshold of life's choices, Nikhilesh invokes Lakshmi—the icon of woman as wife—in his admiration of cousin Munu, who suffers daily the abuses of an alcoholic husband: "O pristine, the dust of your pristine feet has not disappeared from the world completely" (34).

This is perhaps not very surprising. Short, quasi-religious verse narratives extolling the virtues of the ideal Hindu wife sanctioned and iconised by the goddess herself, *Lakshmi Bratakathas*, begin to appear in Bengal from the middle of the eighteenth century. The proliferation of the narratives of the ideal wife as sanctioned by upper-caste Hindu quasi-religious texts coincides with the period when gender relations were being reconstructed within the complex web of patriarchy, imperialism, caste mobility as provided by the census operations of the colonial government, and nationalism between the late nineteenth and early twentieth century in Bengal. A public debate over the condition of women, their physical and social seclusion, their right to live and be after the death of the husband, their right to education, the extent and purpose of such an education, their marriageable age and marital relations—in short, the range of normal subject positions that women could inhabit was the preoccupation of metropolitan Bengal at this historical juncture.

This intense preoccupation with female nature, education, and work was, of course, an elite prerogative. The comparative evaluation of the state of Hindu women, the access to a different norm of conjugality, and the awareness of the need to educate women if one sought companionship, however limited, in one's own wife was greatly influenced by English education. The conservative hysteria, as is manifested by the prolific production of booklets such as the *Lakshmi Bratakatha*s from the middle of the nineteenth century, about the imminent danger to society in its deviation from the ideals of Hindu womanhood is a measure of the stringency of the upper-caste gender norms:

> Their own religion and upbringing they now abdicate
> For an alien religion and knowledge that they wish to accumulate...

The virtues of women, shame and modesty, they kill
These women go every where of their own free will.
The incense and the lamp are not lit when it's dark
The symbol of the good wife, vermillion, their foreheads does not mark.[5]

This is an excerpt from the *Bratakatha* of Lakshmi, which acquires a standardised format by the late nineteenth century. The quasi-religious genre in mapping feminine virtues obviously addresses an anxiety that can be located within the specific context of its articulation, that is, the preoccupation with gender reform. Yet, despite the revivalist attack on the reformist gender norms, dislodging for women the centrality of the household that had been constructed by patriarchal logic was not the agenda of the advocates of female education and emancipation. Even a cursory look at some of the topics discussed in the leading "progressive" journals and conduct books for women of the period reveal that female education was for the express purpose of enabling the woman to discharge her domestic duties better, rather than propel her to choose a life of public duties over private domestic concerns, for "The happiness of the household is entirely dependent upon the grihini (housewife). The dexterity of the grihini, made in the image of Lakshmi, can remove all that is gloomy, soiled and tarnished...."[6] Grihalakshmi, the Lakshmi of the household, became a cryptic cultural code for the steadfast Hindu wife who was idealised as an index of the colonised civilisation in opposition to the colonising West which was then not only different but also degenerate.[7] Ramendrasundar Trivedi's *Banga Lakshmir Bratakatha* (1906) used this trope of Lakshmi to suggest the importance of a national consciousness.[8] On the sixteenth of October 1906, this text was read out in a gathering of thousand women in Jamohandir village in the Murshidabad district of West Bengal. Several nationalistic-swadeshi enterprises used Lakshmi as a suffix. The cotton mill of the Nandi family was called 'Banga Luxmi' and Saraladevi Chaudhurani's swadeshi store was 'Lakshmi Bhandar'.[9] This foregrounding of the Hindu woman in anti-colonial nationalism lent them a certain moral authority, but was not meant to free them entirely from the fetishised norms of wifehood for she was still "to light the unfluttering flame of the softly glowing evening lamp".[10] Thus dovetailed to the tradition of the chaste Hindu woman, Bharati, the nascent modern nation, was already impaled upon the patriarchal dissemination of the Hindu myths of woman as wife.

Yet, the epithets and associations of Sri and Lakshmi in the fifth *Mandala*, 50th *Mantra* of the *Rg Veda,* which is known as the *Sri Sukta,* suggest deities not of the conjugal household but of fertility and vegetation. Vishnu finds no mention here, the goddesses are not wives.[11] According to Suvira Jaiswal, although there are a few references to the wives of some gods in the Vedic literature, the custom of providing every male deity with a female consort representing his shakti or energy and modelled in his image seems to have come in vogue not much before the Gupta period, which gave the mother goddesses attributes of the major gods of the Brahminical pantheon.[12] Lakshmi appears for the first time in association with Vaishnavite symbols on the Gupta coins.[13] The *Puranas, Ramayanas, Mahabharatas*, the *Mangalkabyas* (the popular Bengali compositions between the fifteenth and the eighteenth centuries) and the countless retellings contributed to propagating and consolidating the lineaments of Lakshmi as the golden woman, the happy wife of Vishnu in the region. It is this Lakshmi, as the wife of Vishnu, who becomes the primary ideal of womanhood. The relationship is of subjugation but appeals to a romantic notion of complementary coupling: "*Sri*, the bride of Vishnu.... He is righteousness, she is devotion, He is the creator, and she is creation. *Sri* is the earth, *Hari* the support of it...She is the creeping vine; and Vishnu the tree round which she clings. *Hari* is all that is called male: Lakshmi is all that is termed female: there is nothing else than they".[14] The representative verse from *The Vishnu Purana* extols the happy coupling and glosses the inequality of the relationship which always grants primacy to Vishnu as the male power and the husband. The complementary terms of the romantic coupling are also insidiously suggestive of hierarchy. Descriptions of relationships in a religious text are also prescriptions for right conduct. The patriarchal myth's enduring attraction cannot be understood fully when isolated from the entwined hierarchical caste assumptions of the pure and the polluted measured in terms of their women's codes of conduct. This is how good women of the approved caste Hindu tradition are expected to be. It is this tradition of female existence that is harnessed to the cause of nationalism in the nineteenth century in Bengal that flattens other norms of female existence in other social groups and even within Hinduism.[15] The pedestal is not, however, far from the pit as feminist readings of the representations of the "angel in the house" from several forms of patriarchies have shown.[16] The wife conforming to the sanctioned domestic arrangements will be revered, but only as far as she submits to the norms ordained by patriarchy, caste, class, and other social systems of difference masquerading as natural or divinely ordained hierarchy.

The nineteenth- and early twentieth-century bhadralok family in Bengal is a moment in history where a recognition of the caste-patriarchal gender norms as not a monolith, perfectly stable and uncontested, takes place. The domestic dystopias sketched by the newly empowered women of the upper class and castes sharpened the struggle for social and legal sanctions and/or implementations for its disruption. It is a fraught period when traditional caste-patriarchy is contested. But limits are also re-negotiated. The fictional Nikhilesh, liberal, Western educated, aware of the ills of his country, and good intentioned still recognises the need for male control over gender reforms: "I have made the lamp that lights the home into a fire that razes it. No more indulgence, the time has come to disregard her" (88). The spectrum of Nikhilesh's emotions, from encouragement to anguish, is representative of the scope and limit of the reformist gender project of the period. It is significant that tortured by the vision of the liminal in the re-formation of gendered practices, Nikhilesh turns away from his errant wife Bimala to his cousin Munu and his young and widowed sister-in-law as representing the solace of the supposedly stable past, a return to innocence: "Mejoranididi I do wish we could go back to the time when we newly met in this house" (194). But, the attempt to gloss the miseries in the life of the real woman through metaphoric gestures of deification of the feminine as the deity Annapurna, the provider of plenty, is summarily rejected: "Mejorani let out a long sigh and said, 'No brother. I do not wish to be born again as a woman. Let one birth be sufficient for all that I have suffered, must I endure it again?'" (194).

It is true that the cruel coercion that accompanied the metamorphosis of real women into iconic goddesses had begun to be recognised. Rabindranath Tagore himself was one of the most moving and prolific writers of this theme:

> ...This is good and that's bad, whatever people said with down cast eyes, the veil drawn across my head I survived in this home of yours, for twenty two years no wonder everywhere *Laksmi-Sati*, she is rather a dear; they say of me I hear.
>
> I came to this household a girl just nine following since then the family's long narrow track heaped-demands-bundled on the back dragging all the way I have reached the journey's end today...
>
> (Rabindranath Tagore *Mukti*, 1918)[17]

But the end of the road cannot be envisaged, or accepted so easily and certainly not within that very caste and class who are the custodians of Hindu tradition.

It is her location in history that offers Bimala the possibility of an alternative life outside ghare—the gendered private quarters. Rupture, as always, is heady and fraught with the possibility of devastation and failure. Yet it contains the promise of life.

> The roar of *Bande Mataram* kept coming closer and closer, there is a tremor inside my heart. Suddenly the group of turbaned, saffron clad, bare footed youth and boys entered our huge courtyard like the saffron water of the first rain of the season flooding the dry river ...*Bande Mataram*! *Bande Mataram*! *Bande Mataram*! It seemed as though the sky will be torn asunder" (21).

Is it only a coincidence that Tagore in this passages makes Bimala use the moving metaphor of rain as flooding a parched river? A flooded river does contain the promise of new life, but its overflowing the bank also contains a threat of destruction.

Bankimchandra Chattopadhyay's *Bande Mataram*, glorifying the country as a powerful mother, became a cultic mantra only during the heady days of swadeshi.[18] The Bengali words in the song rendered it accessible while the Sanskrit words infused it with a religiosity that sanctioned militant action:

> *...abala keno ma eto bale|*
> *bahubaladharinig namami taraining*
> *ripudalabarining mataram|*[19]

A pamphlet published in 1905 by Aurobindo Ghosh (1872–1950) proposed the idea of a temple of Bhavani, a militant goddess from the Hindu pantheon, with a celibate order of patriotic devotees vowed to action.[20] "A religious ceremony...such as *Sakti* puja, *Kali* puja and a seditious *katha* or *jatra* and *Swadeshi* conversion... Give a religious turn to the movement. As for the Mohammedans if you can get them on your side why not have a *waz* for boycott and *Swadeshi* preaching..." is what Surendranath Banerjea suggested in 1907 for the anniversary of the boycott that was launched in August 1905 and that officially marked the beginning of the anti-colonial swadeshi movement.[21] This politic metaphor of the nation as mother imbued with militancy and the saviour of the colonised nation swept the imagination of the middle and upper-class Hindu Bengali. The power and popularity of the icon is evident not only in its proliferation in Bengali literature of the period across genres but also in its insertion even in some songs of Rabindranath Tagore and Kaji Nazrul Islam, who were otherwise not brought up on the cult of Shakti.

Yet much of nineteenth-century nationalism that foregrounded the militant mother goddess also celebrated the domestic space as "the Hindu way of life", the autonomous realm of the colonised. The Bengali nationalist discourse that valorised the militant mother also propagated the domestic woman. Bankimchandra Chattopadhyay's cultic *Anandamath* (serialised *chaitra*, 1880, *jaishtha*, 1882, published as a novel, 1882) was the seminal celebration of the militant mother goddess in her new avatar as the enslaved nation demanding freedom. But the same author had also written *Subarnagolak* (1874), a short satire on gender role reversal. Bankimchandra's immensely popular *Devi Chaudhurani* (serialised in 1882–83, published as a novel in 1884) narrates the transformation of the young wife rejected by her polygamous husband's family, because her mother is a poor widow, into a militant saviour goddess of the poor in the colonised nation. The Hindu goddess as militant is the constantly evoked metaphor in the novel. But the potential criticism of the structured domestic life is diffused by the ideological closure, where Devi Chaudhurani reverts to wife Prafulla, recognising that the domestic enclosure is the real arena for feminine fulfilment. Similarly, Michael Madhusudan Dutt's *Virangana Kabya* (1862) and Rabindranath Tagore's *Chitrangada* (1882) explode the masculine-feminine divide and celebrate militant and protesting female characters, using myth as source. Here, too, the closures domesticate the female protagonist's agency or transformative capacity through the evocation of heterosexual love.

The commitment of the bhadralok to swadeshi enabled their women to participate in a political movement. From 1906, educated women began to appear at swadeshi meetings.[22] They contributed ornaments and sang songs. But the possible proximity of men and women outside the home was policed through means such as vows of celibacy and the extension of kinship terms. Sarada Chakrabarty, who started a women's wing, was thought to have misconducted himself in this regard and was consequently put to death in July 1912.[23] Thus, while the moral/religious framework of the nationalist movement enabled women to spill onto public spaces, hitherto a taboo in the patriarchal paradigm, the domestic arena was still retained as the site for the social production of the good and bad women. This deployment was facilitated by the systemic availability of the militant goddesses as wife in hegemonic Hinduism. The resplendent anthropomorphic icon of the mother goddess Durga during the most popular modern festival of the Bengali Hindu—the autumnal *Durga puja*—aggressively visiblised the contradiction where the female icon hypostatised in the act of driving a trident into the male *asura* is still a mother as she is flanked by her four children, with a benign husband, Siva, placed just above. The asura is marked clearly an outsider by his green or black colour as opposed to the yellow and white of the divine family. In the nationalist discourse, on the one hand, the reified mother was the return of the repressed—the orient feminised in the colonising project—striking back through the female as the terrible, avenging mother goddess. On the other hand this ensured that evil was outside the family and the nation. The myths of Sati and Annapurna had traditionally been pressed into the service of domesticating the militant mother goddess(es). Sati's self-willed death on hearing that her husband was being vilified is the absolute absorption of the female identity in the honour of her marriage. In the myths of Annapurna, the liminal qualities of the warrior goddesses are smothered in the image of the feminine mother as the provider of *anna*, the grain of rice, the staple food of eastern India. Thus the contentious—the woman as warrior—is glossed over as composite, the mother and the wife who take militant action but only to protect the home. In *Ghare Baire,* Sandip organises a Durga puja as a show of strength. The puja fissures the national claims of Sandip's swadeshi movement across religions that leads to communal violence. In this incident, class oppression thickens religious identities as Harish Kundu, the oppressive Hindu zamindar, levies additional cesses for the puja on his peasantry that includes evidently a sizeable number of Muslims and lower-caste Hindus. The play of gender identities here also needs to be recognised. As has been noted earlier, the mother goddess Durga is still a familial figure and the asura is marked clearly an outsider. Female militancy is powerful in vanquishing the enemy from outside. But her own familial role is sacrosanct. Family's complicity with violence is thus always layered with myths of domestic sanctuary and the possibility of female life outside it are either smothered or predicated as the lineaments of evil. Despite the felicitation of the militant mother in the Bengali Hindu culture, the militant goddesses unharnessed by marriage, such as Rana Chandi and Ugra Chandi, still circulated in society as metaphors of "*naitik bandhan sithil*"—a slackening of the moral ties.[24]

The monolithic nationalistic history of Bengal (and India) in the late nineteenth and early twentieth centuries is beginning to be read not only as the binary opposition between the coloniser and the colonised but also as the histories of sectarian usurpation of power by the colonised, which implodes the national subject in other terms of oppression such as gender, class, and caste. The fiction of *Ghare Baire* is its ideological representation. Sandip aggressively and cynically admits the Hindu interest in a world perceived as a market. Nikhilesh explodes the national subject by inserting class, as his narrative records the epiphanic arrival of Panchu in the dark night of his soul. Bimala's nationalism has the potential for imploding the unified national self (and family) through the insertion of gender.

> The bridegroom is coming to the neighbourhood, his flute is playing, his lights can be seen, in a moment the girls rush out to the rooftops verandahs windows, they are no longer bothered about their veils, and so that day when the flute of the entire nation's groom could be heard how could the women remain occupied still with the household chores!...For so long the world that the heart knew to be one's own and life's rituals, desire and endeavour tried within the set limit to manage and beautify daily, that day its enclosure was not broken but from atop that fence suddenly from the horizon I heard the call distinctly whose meaning was not clear but the heart grew restless (17).

Bimala's world had hitherto been that of "ghare", the inner quarters segregated from the public world "baire" or outside. "Enclosure", "veil", "set limit", "fence" are words with which she articulates this familiar world that had inscribed her life. The metaphor of marriage and the bridegroom are the tutored terms of sanctioned female expectancy from life with which Bimala tries to register the sudden widening of horizon. The rhetorical excesses, the rush of clauses without punctuation, drive home the point of confinement and the exhilarating possibility of freedom. Is this the new woman speech—fashioned by reform and represented through the recent access to writing?

The surviving evidence, fragmented and meagre, suggests that women have often spoken with anger, bitterness, sorrow, and despair of the patriarchal and patrilocal "ghar" that they entered as child brides with virtually no rights. Patrilocal and patriarchal marriage was clearly traumatic for most women even while it appeared the inevitable telos of caste Hindu female life. This trauma can be located in the crevices of the public, male genres in the vernacular too, despite the idealisation of selfless wifely devotion:

> *Ki jani taper bare Hara mileche bar...*
> *Ek Siva thakahe chariya jai ghar*|[25]
> Is this the result of my penance to have a husband like Hara...
> Let Siva stay on his own I will walk out of the home.

Thus Candi, one of the forms of the militant mother goddess of the Hindu pantheon is made to speak in the *Mangalkabya*s of middle Bengal where *Satider Patininda*—the critique of husbands by the Satis—featured regularly. A non-canonised genre such as the *meyeli charas* or verses composed by women and orally recited is also replete with references to the cruelty inscribed within patriarchal marriages:

> *Amli pata dudher sar*|
> *kemne karbe parer ghar*||
> *parer ghar na jamer ghar*|
> *rait na poyaite kame dhar*||
> *caukher pani dardar*|...
> *parer put raisya*|
> *bet mare kaisya*||[26]
> The cream from milk and *Amli*[27] leaves
> In someone else's home how can she live?
> The marital home or the house of death
> where even before its day to work she is set
> and her tears flow from eyes wet.
> The son of a stranger
> harshly canes her.

O parete kalo rang brishti pare jhamjham||
O parete lanka gachti ranga tuktuk kare|
Gunbati bhai amar man keman kare||
E masta thak didi, kende kakiye |
O masete niye jaba palki sajiye||
Har halo bhaja bhaja mas halo dari|
Sadh jaye nadir jale jhap diya padhi||[28]
Across the river the dark clouds pour rain.
Across the river the red chilli tree shines
there is a yearning in my heart, dear brother mine.
In this month *didi*[29], let your tears flow
next month in a splendid palanquin I'll take you.
My bones have become brittle my flesh has withered
I really do feel like just jumping into the river.

But, predominantly oral, pertaining mainly to "female" concerns, the forms such as the *meyeli charas* remained at the margins of histories of literature and society emplotted within caste patriarchy. Nationalism in search of the uncontaminated realm of colonised life and also inspired by the respectability that folk culture was acquiring in the West, did start to seek these out from the late nineteenth century. Rabindranath Tagore was one such votive. But the discontent of the new woman of post-reform Bengal was seldom read alongside these voices or in terms of changing forms of patriarchies; it was mapped more commonly as the rupture between tradition and modernity.

No. *Satitva* is not Bimala's only matrimony despite the fact that the novel opens with a penitent Bimala recalling her mother as the good woman of the Hindu tradition. Bimala as a woman was never totally innocent of the cruel coercion that helped iconise the feminine household deity: "In our family, in this household of pleasures very few wives have received the respect due to a wife. But apparently that is the rule here" (10). She did not naturally or immediately see a god in her husband from the epiphanic moment of her marriage. Her widowed sisters-in-law were living proofs that wives were usually unhappy, that despite prescribed chaste widowhood neither material nor sexual desires die with the husband and that they could only play out their unfulfilled lives within the confinement of ghare—the house. We never meet Nikhilesh's cousin sister, Munu, in the novel. But she appears in Nikhilesh's narrative as well as in Bimala's. The former glorifies Munu's passive acceptance of sufferings in marriage. But Bimala's blood boils at this female fate:

> When my sister-in-law Munu's husband would beat her up in a drunken state, and later howl in regret, vowed never to touch alcohol again, and then sit down with his drink the next evening—my entire being would burn with hatred (68).

Thus speaks Bimala of the same Munu, the household goddess whose "purity" moved her husband. It is her location in history that offers Bimala the possibility of an alternative life to ghare and Bimala, the unfulfilled subject, slips out, manifesting a desire to be in touch with a world beyond, that is baire.

> There is an amazing similarity between the song of my life and the song of the nation... I have looked ahead and seen, my country stands, as though a girl like me. She was in her own courtyard, today suddenly the unknown has beckoned. There was no time for her to think, she is walking ahead in the dark; she did not even have time enough to light a lamp. I know, how her heart heaves in this silent night. I know, her being has rushed where the flute is calling, so that she feels, "as though I have it, as though I have reached, as though I need fear nothing if I walk on with my eyes shut." No, she is no mother. The child must be suckled, the lamp must be lit in the dark, the dust must be swept from the room, these do not strike her. Today she has a tryst (97).

Gender is the social referent for Bimala's nationalism. Here, clearly it is her subjective experience of life as woman, despite her class privilege, despite her individual good fortune of having a mutantly monogamous husband, that draws the fervour for a new social formation in her. A fervour that signifies discontent with life as it is. And the trope that her narrative uses here is not Lakshmi but that of Radha.

Radha is the central icon of Bengal's Vaishnavism, which was spearheaded by the religious reformer Chaitanya (1486–1533) though he was not the originator of the sect in Bengal. He converted people of the lower castes as well as the mercantile communities of the nearby towns on the lower Bhagirath. Chaitanya's Vaishnavism with its emphasis on individual expressions of love and piety rather than an intellectual conviction or inherited status and purity quotient posed a challenge to orthodox Brahminism. It swept through Bengal's lower and middle artisan and cultivating castes as well as numerous high-caste families, shook the Brahminical monopoly on society, and greatly affected the fabric of Bengali life even though eventually it was domesticated within Brahminism. The philosophical discourses canonised criticism and the sanctioned narratives attempt to confine Radha to the custody of metaphysical concepts of *hladini sakti* (a symbol of the soul's passionate devotion to God) and *parakiya prem* (literally "belonging to another"). Yet, Radha remained a powerful trope of female sexuality: a low-caste working woman who must, and does, leave the confines of the house, unhappy in marriage, victim of male desire, exulting in an adult sexual relationship, deserted and discarded. She is a powerful presence who casts her shadow on the pure woman in conjugal custody. Radha is the dichotomous other of Sati/Lakshmi who circumscribe the sanctioned desires of the Hindu women. It is this history and tradition that Bimala chooses to recall for herself and her nation when she says that "This is our land of *Vaishnav padavali*..." (97). It is inevitable that the momentous and exhilarating beginning for Bimala in the political life of her nation is communicated and intermeshed in terms of a sexual experience, and for a while Bimala is drawn as much to the movement as to Sandip. It is also inevitable that Sandip's brazen admissions and Nikhilesh's tortured soliloquies should frame Bimala's nationalism as the politics of passion and destruction.

It is not as though Bimala is incapable of introspection. But Bimala's trajectory is always undermined by the narratives of Nikhilesh and Sandip. The two male narratives manifest patriarchal deployment of binary opposites—ideal/material, mind/body, culture/nature, active/passive—in their construction of Bimala. Thus the male narratives contain and critique Bimala's "truth". In Nikhilesh's words:

> We are men, freedom is our arduous endeavour: we will rush forward at the call of ideals, we have to rescue the captive Lakshmi by scaling the walls of the demon land—the girl who stitches our flag of success with her dexterous hand she is our partner in the religious enterprise. And the one who weaves the web for us in the corner of the house may we know her true identity, pierce her disguise and not send her to dissolve our austere endeavour by bedecking her into a beautiful nymph by the colour of our own desire (114).

The Bimala produced by the contrapuntal male narratives is thus relegated to the realm of the essential feminine. And Bimala's desire? Both Nikhilesh and Sandip are certain that they can read it. For Nikhilesh, " The monstrous appeals to her" (35) and according to Sandip, " She is the avid tongue of the summer storm, red with excitement of secret desire" (52).

Does Bimala support violent Hindu chauvinism and coercion despite her gendered existence? It is her participation in the movement, however limited, that leads her to examine the contradictions of the movement and to attempt to articulate her own position.

> But when this eighteen-year-old boy could feel so easily that to murder a blameless old man is the call of religious righteousness then my whole being shivered.(144)...The next day I met Sandip again. A naked frenzy seized my heart again. But what is this! Is this my nature! Certainly not (145)... I could not distinguish my home from my country! Today I am robbing my home, it amounts to robbing the country—the self same sin made me lose both my home and my country (148)...What am I to them! A wild flower in the face of a flood. But what did Sandip gain in extinguishing me thus? These six thousand rupees? But was there nothing in me worth more than these six thousand rupees? Of course there was. I had heard that from Sandip himself, and it is on hearing that that I had junked everything in my world. I will bring light, I will bring life, I will bring energy, I will bring the elixir of life, it was this faith, this joy that had made me

> rush out in a flood (150)...Today they want to say that it was all a pack of lies?(150)...For a few days I have been feeling that I possess a dual intelligence. One part of my intelligence realizes that this destructive aspect of Sandip is dangerous; another part says but this is so attractive (183).

But the narratives of the two men come together in blocking the potential gender claim in Bimala's narrative, pegging it either as an egoist's dream of mobilising a movement or, more damagingly, locating the repressive social oppressor in her. Nikhilesh says of Bimla:

> Actually Bimal, by nature is what is called a "lady". Even though she comes from a poor background, she is a queen... She knows that the yardstick for measuring the happiness and sorrow, the good and bad of the lower class is for ever of a lower order.... She is truly of Manu's lineage" (91).

In the Hindu religious tradition, *Manusmriti* refers to the well-known collection of laws and precepts, probably held the most sacred after the Vedas. It was formulated between 200 BC and AD 200, and admitted more than one redaction, though the text has been more or less the same from the sixth century onwards. *Vivadarnavasetu* (Bridge Over the Ocean of Disputes), the work on Hindu laws of inheritance, family, etc., compiled by a number of Brahmin *pandits* for Warren Hastings and translated by Nathaniel Brassey Halhed in 1776, depended largely on the *Manusmriti*. Sir William Jones, who had came to India in 1783 as a Judge of the Supreme Court, published his *Manusmriti* in1794. Raja Rammohun Roy, one of the initiators of the gender reform movement in colonial Bengal, invited a sociological and historical approach to the study of *Manusmriti*, especially between 1816 and 1832.[30] *Manusmriti* was a central iconic text in the sanctioning of caste hierarchy and the attendant social repression and political subjugation of women whose chastity ensures the purity of caste lineage. The enlightened Nikhilesh says that the blood of Manu ran in Bimala. She is unable to relate to her social inferiors. Bimala embodies the ideological assertion of exploitation—or so Nikhilesh's narrative would have it.

It needs must be inserted that the judgment on Bimala here is by a zamindar, whose family lives by receiving rent from land cultivated mainly by low-caste Hindu and Muslim peasants possibly since the days of Murshid Quli Khan[31] despite the zamindari going into the hands of the "receivers" thrice.[32] Nikhilesh's sense and sensibilities, not withstanding the tax, wends its way through the *sadar* collected from the ryot, "hungry, tired and emaciated". Nikhilesh's narratives foreground his life as an intellectual interiority glossing the materialistic—urban consumer goods with which he floods his wife, the sea of chrysanthemums in his garden, and his failed swadeshi experiments. Yet, all of it is possible because of the surplus withdrawn from the peasant economy. Nikhilesh nostalgically recalls the romantic boat rides with Bimala in the monsoon month of *Bhadra* when the moon is in its bright phase and when for the peasantry the labour of transplantation of paddy begins. Nikhilesh's romantic season of celebrating his anniversary is called the "*badantor*" or the backbreaker in the peasant vocabulary."[33] The purpose here is not to advocate an aesthetic of praise and blame but to draw attention to the complexity of the text that imbricates its self-same characters as the capillaries of power even as they attempt to move towards freedom.

At the end of the novel, Nikhilesh remains poised between life and death. Bimala contrite, chastened, caves in to the traditional patriarchal construct and is at Nikhilesh's feet. She yearns to return to the stable icon of her childhood, her mother as Sati—the traditional Hindu icon of woman great in her absolute abnegation of her self. Nikhilesh and Bimala do not have lives outside of the text. But the text, through Bimala's experience, has already scripted the inadequacies of the domestic icons, Sati, Lakshmi, Annapurna... They failed to fulfil the female entirely within domesticity. The unfulfilled female subject had slipped out of their grasp, even if for a while in the hope of shaping Bharati—women's viability in the political life of the new nation that is in process. It is her participation in the political life of the nation that makes Bimala empathise with her milkmaid and domestics, Thako and Khemo. A similar possibility of gender solidarity in action is also briefly visible in her sister-in-law's recognition of the denial of right that forces Bimala to steal, a denial that draws the two women together for a brief moment in Mejorani's speech:

> Bimal said, " I have taken out the money"
> I was startled.
> Mejorani asked, " Where have you kept it ?"
> Bimal said, "I have spent it."
> Mejorani said, "My! Just listen to her. How did you spend so much money?"
> Bimal did not answer. I also did not ask her anything else, I just held on to the door and kept quiet. Mejorani was about to say something to Bimal but she checked herself; she looked at me and said, " Its fine if she has taken it. I also used to steal whatever money was left in my husband's pocket and bag. I knew that this money will just be looted by the others. Brother-in-law you are also like that. You know so many ways to waste money on whims. Your money is safe only if we steal it..." (200–01).

The novel had started by distinguishing Nikhilesh from his debauched brothers. It forced a recognition of Bimala's good fortune in that her experience of marriage was so very different from Mejorani's life of deprivation despite her good looks. Yet, towards the end, Mejorani shares with Bimala a sense of gendered exclusion—the wives have no right over finances even in their household.

A sense of tragic failure hangs over the conclusion of the novel. "God can create the new, but does he have the power to create anew from the ruined remains of his creation?"(190). The novel may return Bimala to her husband's feet in ghare. Yet, can it celebrate conjugality as an end in itself and shut out the call of the world outside for women as much for men? Despite the closure, can the novel deny that participation in politics of the new nation in formation holds the promise, however nebulous, of such a condition where women organise themselves, demand suffrage and reform instead of waiting forever for fate?

Notes

1. Rabindranath Tagore, *Ghare Baire,* 1916, Kolkata, Viswabharati, 1994, 22. All future quotations refer to this edition of the text.
2. The *Puranas* represent a corpus composed with a view to widen the social base of Brahminism. These are miscellaneous compendia of myth, ritual, philosophy, history, and religion. There are 18 *Maha Puranas*. The *Puranas* are written at such divergent periods and have undergone, in the great majority of cases, such continual and substantial re-editions accommodating the needs of changing social conditions that scholars find it difficult to fix their chronology. It is accepted, however, that all are later than the epics, with the cores of several being composed during the Gupta period, that is, fourth–fifth centuries AD and most having reached their present state before the twelfth century AD.
3. Tapati Guha-Thakurta, *The Making of a New "Indian" Art: Artists, Aesthetics and Nationalism in Bengal, c.1850–1920,* Cambridge, Cambridge University Press, 1992, 259.
4. For the concept of shakti see Sukumari Bhattacharji, *The Indian Theogony: Brahma, Visnu and Siva,* 1970, Calcutta, Penguin, 2000, 14–15.
5. *Prati Brihaspatibarer Sri Sri Lakshmi Debir Bratakatha,* Kolkata, Orient Library, n.d., 5. Translated from the Bengali. This formulaic narrative is repeated by Bengali women till today in virtually every caste Hindu household on Thursdays.
6. Dinesh Chandra Sen, *Grihasri,* Kolkata, Viswakosh Press, 1915, 1–10.
7. See Aparajita Sengupta, "From Nation to Gender: Identity, Order and Women in Nationalistic Thought in Late 19th and early 20th Century Bengal" in Ranjit Kumar Roy, ed., *Retrieving Bengal's Past: Society and Culture in the 19th and 20th Century,* Calcutta, Rabindra Bharati University, 1995, 60–76. Tanika Sarkar, *Hindu Wife, Hindu Nation,* New Delhi, Permanent Black, 2001. Dipesh Chakrabarty, "The Difference-Deferral of (A) Colonial Modernity : Public Debates on Domesticity in British Bengal", *History Workshop Journal,* no. 36, 1993, 1 34.
8. Ramendrasundar Trivedi, *Bangalakkhir Bratakatha* in Barunkumar Chakrabarty and Dibyajyoti Majumdar, eds., *Banglar Loksamskriti,* 1906, Calcutta, Aparna Book Distributors, 1996. Translated from the Bengali.

9. Omkar Goswami, "Sahibs, Babus and Banias: Changes in Industrial Control in Eastern India 1918–50" in Rajat Kanta Ray, ed., *Entrepreneurship and Industry in India 1800–1947,* Delhi, Oxford University Press, 1992, 249.
10. Indira Devi, "Adarsha", *Sabujpatra,* IInd year, numbers 5 & 6, Kolkata, 1915. Translated from the Bengali.
11. It belongs to the *Khila Sukta* section, the late supplementary 15 verses appended to the regular collection of the hymns of the *Rg Veda* (though the number of *mantras* constituting the *Sri Sukta* differs from one recension to the other). Sashibhushan Dasgupta, *Sri Radhar Kromobikas* (1952, Calcutta: A.Mukherji & Co, 1963), 16. Sukumari Bhattacharya, *The Indian Theogony,* 1970, New Delhi, Penguin India 200, 359.
12. Suvira Jaiswal, *The Origin and Development of Vaisnavism (200BC–500AD),* Delhi, Munshiram Manoharlal, 1980, 110–14.
13. A gold coin depicting Lakshmi on a throne, belonging to Samudragupta (AD 330–375) was discovered from Burdwan's Barari village in Bengal. Nripendra Bhatta, *Lakshmi Asa Theke Asvine,* Calcutta, Manalok, 1964, 15.
14. H.H.Wilson, trans., *The Vishnu Purana: System of Hindu Mythology and Tradition,* Calcutta, Punthi Pustak, 1961, 52–53.
15. Desire for caste mobility also helped homogenise the icon of Lakshmi as feminine fulfilment in domestic wifedom. Gender rights are often the first casualties of sanskritisation. The articulation of the Candal defiance of the caste authority of 1872–73 in Bengal, for instance, also curbed their women's right to visit the market places in imitation of the upper-caste practices of segregated spheres of gender activities and the privileging of the home for women. Sekhar Bandyopadhyay, *Caste, Politics and the Raj: Bengal 1872–1937,* Calcutta, 1990, 98.
16. The phrase, specifically referring to a Victorian ideal, is actually the title of a popular poem of the mid-1850s by Coventry Patmore.
17. Rabindranath Tagore, *Sancaita,* 1931, Viswabharati, Santiniketan, 1958, 553. Translated from the Bengali.
18. "The miraculous transformation of *Bande Mataram* from an innocent song into a revolutionary slogan was the work of young Bengal of 1905" Haridas Mukherjee and Uma Mukherjee, ed., *Bande Mataram And Indian Nationalism 1906–8,* Calcutta, Firma KLM, 1957, 10.
19. Bankimchandra Chattopadhyay, *Ananadamath, Bankim Racanabali-Upanyasa Samagra,* Calcutta, Punascha, 2000, 625.

20. Rajat Kanta Ray, *Social Conflict and Political Unrest in Bengal. 1875–1927,* Delhi, OUP, 1984, 141.
21. Ibid., 166.
22. Ibid., 161.
23. Ibid.,185.
24. Kunjabihari Basak, *Sansar Chitra*, Calcutta, 1899, 59.
25. Sukumar Sen, ed., *Kabikankan birachit Chandimangal,* 1975, New Delhi, Sahitya Akademi, 1993, 27.
26. Ashutosh Bhattacharya, *Banglar Lok Sahitya*, volume II, *Chara,* Calcutta: Calcutta Book House, 1963, 373.
27. In villages the leaves of this plant are ground and given to young children to protect them from cold.
28. Anathnat Das and Biswanath Roy, ed., *Rabindranath Thakur Abanindranath Thakur Sam Grihit Chelebhulan Chara,* Calcutta, Ananda Publishers Pvt. Ltd., 1995, 314.
29. A term for elder sister in Bengali.
30. Parnasabari Bhattacharya, *Conceptualizing in the Manusmriti,* New Delhi, Manohar, 1996, 2.
31. He was appointed as Dewan in November 1700 by Aurangazeb.
32. Nikhilesh's grandmother mentions that she has seen the property go to the "receivers" thrice in her lifetime. This is quoted in the context of the grandmother's refusal to admonish Nikhilesh's extravagant ways in Bimala's opening narrative (18). For an explanation of the term "receiver" see Sharmila Purkayastha's article.
33. Radhakamal Mukherji, *The Changing Face of Bengal: A Study in Riverine Economy,* Calcutta, University of Calcutta, 1938, 45.

6

Beyond the Intricate Web of Words: An Essay on Tagore's *Ghare Baire*

SHIRSHENDU CHAKRABARTI

I

In his writings on the Western-educated urban middle classes in Bengal, Tagore reiterates the breakdown of conjugal ties, the trauma and loneliness of women and their darker sexual intensities. In his novels and shorter fiction—his short stories do not really concentrate on the urban middle-class milieu—Tagore's women struggle to make sense and take control of their lives on the brink of hysteria and madness. *Nashtaneed, Ghare Baire, Chaturanga, Jogajog* are some well-known examples of jeopardised domesticity. In this respect, Tagore is a legatee of Bankimchandra Chattopadhyay, who had established in his domestic fiction the paradigm of transgressive, often self-destructive, passion within a middle-class milieu in the latter half of the nineteenth century. Thus, the mad woman who was discovered in the attic of the Victorian home by recent Western scholarship already occupied centre stage in modern Bengali fiction—in Tagore she was usually the heroine.

If the novel in Bengal (and India) came into being as a product of colonial education, then where did this paradigm of passion come from? After all, barring a few exceptions, the Victorian domestic novel is marked by settled family life and the prudential distrust of ungovernable passion. Of course, the Bengali novelist could draw upon other European sources: despite being steeped in classical Sanskrit literature, Bankim nevertheless chose to go, for instance, to Shakespeare in search of tempestuous, tragic passion. While Victorian domestic fiction may not have inspired the Bengali novelist, Victorian values were a visible "civilizing/colonizing" influence on the Bengali middle classes, moulding in particular the ideals of companionate marriage, family and home. Thus Victorian morality gave rise to a new concept of domesticity, but fictional representation of that domesticity exposed the stifling hypocrisy and limitations of that morality. Victorian values may have introduced the notion of companionate marriage to the middle-class Hindu household, but the entire process involved a poeticisation and aestheticisation of woman: a prosaic and routine domesticity is turned into a sanctimonious ideal by a rhetoric of mystification that straddles both the home and the world.

Focussing on this mystification of woman in *Ghare Baire* (1916), Tagore exposes the interlocked combat of domination and submission underlying it. In search of truth and freedom from this inner war of deception and self-deception, Tagore surrounds the intricate and interwoven structure of words (the monologues) with the muted but dignified suffering of teeming millions. When Nikhilesh is able to place himself within this vast manifold, he is, as it were, emancipated from his typically middle-class (or upper-class) absorption in personal grief. Monologic introspective subtlety finds dialogic extension in the almost silent but haunting presence of the famished, toiling classes. In fact, this dialogic model shapes the basic structure of many of Tagore's novels. In *Gora*, the protagonist actually discovers and identifies himself precisely with the *Bharatvarsha* of the *shudra* (and not of the bhadralok) that Nikhilesh speaks of, and in *Chaturanga*, the feeding of shudras and Muslims is equated with serving God. These novels are all centred around eloquent debates, but beyond the aggressive eloquence there is a whole world uncontaminated and unfettered by the aggrandising, often calculating egoism, of the emerging middle classes. It is not a coincidence that Nikhilesh's attempts to break out of this egoism brings him to the simple truth of Nature which invites both a parallel and ironic contrast with the life of deprivation.

In *Ghare Baire* (1916), appropriately enough, Tagore begins with the older form of domesticity, locating it in a zamindari household governed, as Bimala says, by the dictates of Manu and Parashar on the one hand, and those of the Moghuls and Pathans on the other. In this older system, the home and the world are kept apart, clearly divided between women and men: the dissipated routine of husbands away from home renders the domestic space emotionally and sexually stifling for wives. Both the elder brothers of Nikhilesh, we are told, have drunk themselves to untimely death. Of course, Nikhilesh does not feel the need for alcohol or other excesses of appetite, but then his sobriety and rationalism are not unrelated to the fact that he belongs to the new age and is the first in his family to receive an English education. His stability is frowned upon by the women of the household, because it challenges that demarcation of home and the world wherein the women, at times with servile cunning, could control the domestic space by allowing unbridled freedom to men in the world. The two sisters-in-law of Bimala significantly cling on to this spurious conjugal arrangement and a life of bleak confinement indoors, because allegiance to rank and family prestige is the only basis of their identity. By contrast to this older conformity, historical change manifests itself in the defiance or rebellion of many of Tagore's upper-class heroines.

The older mode of domesticity was, of course, not always so unhappy or oppressive: Bimala recalls her mother's role as a devoted wife. But she simultaneously realises that the unaffected, self-effacing simplicity of that domestic routine is beyond recovery. In her interior monologue (atmakatha) with which *Ghare Baire* opens, Bimala examines her location within a domestic space suddenly destabilised by historical change. As the widely acknowledged legatee of her mother, Bimala discovers that the humdrum domesticity of the immediate past was being supplanted by a poeticised and mystified version. As I have indicated above, the underlying manipulative ideology affects both the home and the larger world. Without being aware of it, Bimala is trapped between rival projects of domination: on the one hand, Nikhilesh attempts to mould her into an enlightened, Western-educated wife-companion; on the other hand, Sandip appropriates her for the political cult of the Mother Goddess. It is no wonder that Chandranath Babu, Nikhilesh's old teacher, discovers a strange affinity between Nikhilesh and Sandip and describes the latter as a kind of *doppelganger* of the former.

In the short passage of time from adolescence to youth, Bimala feels she has been propelled suddenly to an entirely new age by the upsurge of swadeshi fervour, which is compared to the excitement produced among home-bound women by the arrival of the bridegroom for a wedding. Once the continuity between the past and the present is violently broken, Bimala loses her location within a stable domestic sphere. As she looks back at her wifely devotion from the other side of the divide between the old and the new, she realises that this devotion has been invested with a poeticised and specious beauty. She perceives in public opinion an admonition:

> to mould that which was as easy as breathing into a poetic art. The imaginatively inclined men of today are raising their pitch constantly as they hold forth on the unparalleled poetry of the wifely devotion of married women and abstinence of widows. It is evident from this how in this domain of life there has been a breach between truth and beauty.[1]

Thus, freedom from traditional domesticity exposes Bimala and the new woman to the manipulative strategies of middle-class ideology which reinvents her as an aesthetic object. That the enlightened Nikhilesh is unconsciously complicit with this disguised exercise of power is part of the subtle and self-critical irony of the entire novel. Bimala senses this in the way her capacity for love is smothered by Nikhilesh's lavish display of affection. Her situation may remind us of Monimalika in Tagore's well-known short story *Monihara* (1898), written almost two decades before *Ghare Baire*. We have the familiar upper-class milieu and the Western-educated husband who, in his pursuit of companionate marriage, systematically adorns his wife with ornaments. The wife does not respond or reciprocate because she only receives and is unable to give anything back. She is childless and becomes frighteningly, almost insanely possessive about her ornaments. Like her, Bimala also passively receives without being actively able to give back anything. This denial suggests an aesthetic moulding, precisely the beauty that has been ruptured from truth: "After all, love is by nature unworldly; it grows its flowers in profusion on the dust by the road, but it cannot spread its riches in a china vase in the drawing-room" (475).

Nikhilesh dresses up Bimala in the latest English fashions, teaches her English, and even appoints an English woman as a kind of governess. Although his grandmother does not approve of these measures, she accepts them, because according to her traditional perspective in the matter, if Nikhilesh had not decked up his wife he would have decked up a concubine. Such is the depth of self-deception that in explaining female pettiness in terms of the cramped feet of Chinese women, Nikhilesh is unaware of the ironic link in his chosen example between beauty and domination. He is similarly unaware of the darker intensities seething under domestic routine and is totally unprepared for the outburst of adulterous passion. Actually, the aestheticisation of woman presupposes absorption with individualism, with an intensely narrow focus on personal grief or happiness. Even Nikhilesh's initially abrupt and devastating clarity of vision that exposes the hollowness of his entire conjugal life is not free from the disillusionment that accompanies such self-absorption. But from his second monologue onwards he begins to find the secret of release from personal tragedy in solidarity with the vast concourse of teeming millions through the ages.

As Nikhilesh identifies himself with the ongoing stream of life, he realises how narrow and transient his desire to possess Bimala is. Bimala is his wife, but she has an identity of her own, and it is impossible to stuff and then lock up an entire human being inside the word "wife". He had attempted to suppress her objective entity under some lofty ideals of his own imagination, but, in the process, he has enslaved himself to this mental image. In his final monologue, after he discovers that Bimala has removed six thousand rupees from the strongbox, Nikhilesh understands the tyranny underlying the education of a companionate wife:

> Since my desire has been to cast my relationship with Bimal into a mould of rigid goodness without a blemish, it has an element of coercion in it. But human life cannot be cast into a mould. If you try to shape goodness as though it were something inert, it takes terrible revenge by dying at once. Because of this tyranny, deep within we have moved away unknowingly from each other. What Bimal could have become by herself could not blossom forth because of my dead weight ... There are those who get along with people like us, single-minded in our ideas, but those who do not get along cheat us. We turn guileless people deceitful. In order to fashion a conjugal companion we disfigure a wife (590).

Above all, Nikhilesh realises that the desire to dominate is inseparable from the desire to be dominated, that these twin impulses are interchangeable and interlinked. If Bimala expresses her impulse to power through Sandip's politics of rapacity cloaked in a heady rhetoric of nationalist zeal, she simultaneously surrenders herself to his aggressive masculinity. We may also recall that after her grand-mother-in-law's death, she refuses Nikhilesh's offer to shift to Calcutta because of the power and prestige attached to the ancestral seat. When the servant, under instructions from Bimala's sisters-in-law, stops Sandip from meeting her and is therefore slapped by him, the latter's overweening attitude finds a parallel in her reactions. The Miss Gilby episode is yet another instance of her impulse to exercise her power.

It is the desire to dominate and be dominated that enables Sandip to appropriate Bimala as the mother goddess. She believes that men must see in women the specific form of the goddess of shakti. This picture of woman, however, actually reduces her to the stereotype of the bewitching enchantress whose power to bewitch springs from her dependence on male fantasy and desire. That is why the rhetoric of nationalism and female shakti, exchanged between Sandip and Bimala is contaminated by furtive, manipulative sexuality—consider, for instance, Sandip's gushing and rarefied "poetry," involving fire, stars, and similar cosmic energies, directed at Bimala's fashionable clothes, that is, at woman as an aesthetic object or consider the frissons of eroticism obliquely introduced through literature and art. In fact, if on the superficial level Sandip disrupts middle-class domestic order, on an ideologically treacherous level he reinforces it.

On a larger scale, the intermeshing of power and servitude is a product of history that is being ideologically consolidated by Sandip's brand of "swadeshi", for the psychology that drives the bhadralok to challenge his colonial master is actually a servile greed for power over the deprived masses. As Nikhilesh puts it, "from gods to policemen our country has feared so many and for so long that it is now only half-alive", and it is fear of the same bugbear that finds expression in political intimidation of the helpless in the name of swadeshi (549). The hardening and warping that aestheticisation presupposes is seen clearly in political life where the ability to oppress, to be ruthless, and to kill one's human instincts is being glorified. This certainly is part of the indoctrination of the activist who has an M.A. in history. The rhetoric of strong and harsh authority is founded on the psychology of servitude. Nikhilesh's rebuttal of the arguments of the M.A. in history brings this out clearly in both the home and the world:

> When the poison of servitude that is ingrained in our marrow gets an opportunity to surface, it then takes the form of a dangerous oppression. The same woman who is persecuted as a wife turns into the biggest persecutor as a mother-in-law (550).

In attempting to mould Bimala's personality according to his own lofty ideals, Nikhilesh enslaves himself. Consequently, in his fifth monologue, in which he encounters the lonely and disconsolate

Bimala in the inner garden of chrysanthemums, Nikhilesh decides not to bind her by force to marital ties since that would put his own life in fetters: "I shall not find release if I do not release her." The ultimate freedom is the freedom from desire, for desire traps us into the pursuit of power:

> the day I can really release the bird from its cage I will realize that it is the bird who releases me. The one I bind in a cage binds me in my desire and that is bondage stronger than that of chains (552).

Nikhilesh's absorption in personal grief is symptomatic of middle-class individualism; by contrast, the starving poor do not have even the time for indulgence in melancholy, for bloating it out of all proportion. In the world inhabited by Bimala, woman's sorrow is nothing new, what is new is the poeticisation of this sorrow. This exercise is crucial to Sandip's philosophy of aggressive appetite according to which the stereotypical male causes pain in women which the latter have learned to relish, desire, and cherish. Once again, the interlocking of sadism and masochism makes the human psyche a meeting point of power and subjugation:

> If we had not always made women cry, then the door would never have opened on to their stored wealth of sorrow... [Bimala] had been waiting for me because till now she had not been able to cry properly. Because till now she had lived only in happiness, the moment she saw me, the dark early monsoon clouds of sorrow gathered on her heart's horizon (542).

The entire exercise of aestheticisation/poeticisation in the novel is sustained through rhetoric. As I have already argued, Sandip's manipulative rhetoric is stamped with rapacity. He chooses to manipulate language because he believes that words cover up and render acceptable what is at bottom mere predatory appetite, universally applicable. According to him, people want to follow the dictates of this appetite and actually follow them but they must hide it in lofty words in order to deceive others and in the process they deceive themselves. Everything for Sandip is driven by the greed for power and there is some truth in this exposure of the savagery implicit in civilisation. That Tagore was not unaware of this can be seen clearly in his celebrated poem *Prithibi* (*Earth*). But submission to this truth involves a submission to blind biological forces (a kind of Darwinism, perhaps), to a loss of human freedom. These blind biological drives become elemental energies under Sandip's rhetoric and associated with the stereotype of female shakti/Mother Goddess: modern biology and tantric doctrine become interchangeable. But Sandip confesses to chinks in his libertinist armour when he realises that his philosophy is also a construction and therefore a self-imposed yoke: his relationship with Bimala begins to go beyond his strategies of calculation. Here again he is Nikhilesh's doppelganger, trying to shape his whole life in strict accordance with a set of ideas and then discovering that he has been partly constructed before he began his self-construction. This is clearly revealed in his third monologue when he wonders if he is made of words:

> When I read my autobiography, I wonder, "Is this Sandip? Am I made of words? Am I a book bound by flesh and blood?" (517).

If Sandip is a servant of predatory appetite, Nikhilesh is in his turn a servant of the obverse, that is, the life-long attempt to master appetite. Rational self-control isolates Nikhilesh in a kind of coldness, in an avowed incapacity for moving others; by contrast, while Bimala arouses Sandip's lust and instinct for domination, Amulya is truly inspired by her. Self-control is of course the obverse of control, inviting a parallel with aestheticisation. It had stifled Nikhilesh's expressive freedom and through the crisis of the novel he moves towards the recovery of this freedom. In his fourth monologue Nikhilesh realises that Bimala has dressed up with special care in order to entice him to remove English clothes from the market. When this oppressive measure is defended by Bimala on the grounds that it is for the sake of the country, Nikhilesh refuses her bluntly: "Oppression for the sake of the country is oppression on the country, you will not understand this." At once he experiences an illuminating sense of unburdening, an irresistible freedom: a vast delight from the depths of his being suddenly touches the clouds like a waterspout (537). In his fifth monologue when he defines emancipation from desire, even his teacher, Chandranath Babu, is taken aback by his emotional excitement.

We may recall that the first hypnotic influence that Sandip has on Bimala is through the tumid rhetoric of his address to his followers. In a sense, all the three characters in the novel are made of words and that is one of the reasons why Tagore chose the specific form of this novel. Nikhilesh speaks in riddling similies and symbols and struggles to move beyond the obsessive personal grief that he spins around himself with words. The whole process of poeticisation/aestheticisation is immersed in words. In her very first monologue, Bimala discovers that even as she tries to describe the domestic happiness of the past, the language of today, in which she has been informally educated, comes in her way turning straightforward prose into poetry.

Introspective eloquence is subtly linked to the lack of productive work both at home and in the world. While her sisters-in-law are located within a domestic routine of chores or rituals, Bimala is rarely shown in a situation of work. Not only is the entire programme of swadeshi critiqued by Chandranath Babu and Nikhilesh in terms of its alienation from any constructive activity, but the resulting destructiveness also fuels the rhetoric of shakti. Community worship of shakti in the form of the Goddess Durga is also related to the lack of actual shakti among the Bengali middle classes. No doubt Nikhilesh has been engaged in practical work in the past—Chandranath Babu gives a whole list of these activities—but they have all been failures. His failure puts the question of productive labour in its proper historical perspective: in a colonial economy, the Bengali middle classes did not really have the freedom to engage in such activity. Their alienated existence placed them in a strange situation of ruling over the productive masses, but always within a colonial administration, that is, always without real power and therefore hankering after it.

The mode of the atmakatha is thus not unrelated to this historical vacuum occupied by the middle classes. Its psychological tortuosities and intrusive uncertainties spin a web of words wherein the rationalising characters are somewhat trapped even as language remains the specific tool of self-questioning that can potentially lead to self-knowledge. Inner anxiety surfaces as endless debate and argument, and the whole novel is, like many other novels of Tagore, riddled with debate. Around the dominant structure of debate, however, there is a muted presence of matter-of-fact simplicity. Verbal dexterity is used in this novel, as elsewhere in his work, as a mirror of the cobwebs that we spin around us, particularly if we are alienated from productive functions in society. The dexterity unfolds itself to the point of exhaustion, on the margins of which we are able to grasp the simplicity that lies beyond it. For the upper-class characters, there is no other route to this simplicity because the intricate sophistry of desire cannot be by-passed.

In her first monologue, Bimala speaks of a devotional simplicity which we may relate to Tagore's larger use of *bhakti* in his poetry. Is this a nostalgic escape from modern reality? As I see it in relation to the sustained examination of truth in the novel and indeed the entire work of Tagore, it offers an alternative to a mode of deliverance from the lack of clarity that accompanies the interlinked pursuit of power and servitude, from the additives of heady rhetoric that we submit ourselves to in order to remain secure.

At first the idea of a simple truth emerges out of the debate about swadeshi and aestheticisation. Bimala, we may recall, notices a breach between truth and beauty in the domestic sphere, giving rise to false notions of beauty involving particularly the wife, the widow, and sexual abstinence. In the political world, the breach is manifest in the inability to perceive the country as a plain and prosaic reality. When in Bimala's first monologue, Nikhilesh cautions Sandip against worshipping one's country as God, he does it from the conviction that truth and *dharma* are above everything and they must not be clouded by the self-deluding magic spell of nationalist rhetoric. According to Sandip, however, what is true is the identity of God and country: the God he worships is incarnate in human beings and in one's own country. But in that case, as Nikhilesh reminds him, there should be no disparity between one human being and another and therefore between one country and another: how can hatred of English rule and of the English people be sustained from this position? By turning the country into God, the swadeshi activists defend their tyranny over their starving fellow countrymen, but such duplicity becomes possible precisely because we cannot accept truth without intoxicants. At this point, Bimala intervenes in the debate by asserting that the history of civilised nations like Britain, France, Germany, and Russia offers ample evidence of this duplicity, this "theft." As Sandip defends her position, Nikhilesh draws our attention to the warping and deeply corrosive effect of rapacious nationalism on the soul of aggressive civilisations. In its heyday of prosperity and opulence, the Roman civilisation became morally bankrupt but the degeneration was not evident from the outside. This is the fate of the formidable predatory civilisations.

When, in the fourth monologue of Nikhilesh, the zealous "swadeshi" activists under the leadership of Sandip demand that all English products be removed from the markets in Nikhilesh's area, the latter refuses because the poor will suffer. When the activists retort that this suffering is for the country, Chandranath Babu exposes the inhumanity underlying their patriotism. Swadeshi actually borders upon a middle-class fad that does not require any sustained practical activity since the economic consequences, say, of boycotting and burning foreign clothes are almost entirely borne by the poor. As he reminds the activists, the country that they supposedly worship involves the survival and happiness of its teeming poor. They have never bothered even to look at the abject poverty of the latter and now they want to dictate to them what salt they should eat and what clothes they should wear. When the activists reply that they have themselves begun using swadeshi salt, sugar, and clothes, Chandranath Babu exposes their sacrifice as an affordable whim that satisfies their vanity. We learn further that Nikhilesh has in fact stocked swadeshi goods in his markets and even sent them to the neighbouring areas. The activists themselves concede that despite this availability no one is buying these goods. So the problem is not with Nikhilesh's market but because the country as a whole has not accepted the mission of swadeshi. Consequently, the whole affair turns out to be a sordid and short-sighted exercise in exploitation in the name of patriotic fervour. In his very first monologue, Nikhilesh had reminded himself that the need for an illusion or intoxicant over and above the plain truth is a sign of our ingrained slavishness. In order to keep going we need a master in some form, whether it is an idea or the conservative Hindu code or even an individual.

On a far deeper level the notions of simplicity and truth are suggested by the almost silent presence of the world of Panchu surrounding the eloquence of the monologues. In his third monologue, Nikhilesh senses that he is on the brink of understanding his situation involved with that of the others and the whole country. He realises that the love between man and woman has been blown unmanageably out of proportion and must be cut down to size. It is thus not a coincidence that his personal grief, awakened by the empty bedroom with all its furniture and things and by the brief meeting with Bimala, takes him instinctively to Amiel's journal (a mode similar to that of the atmakatha). But the encounter with Panchu, which immediately follows, liberates him from the tyranny of introspective uncertainty. This man, who has to toil all day for an occasional square meal, has come to return the few coconuts he had once stolen from Nikhilesh's orchard: death being a perpetual possibility in his life, he does not want to remain in debt for long. At once Nikhilesh's mind is cleansed of its inbred, ingrown sorrow and he realises that the world extends far beyond the joy and pain of union with and separation from a particular woman. Human life is vast in its range and scope and in order to measure our individual happiness and sorrow we must stand in its midst. Each individual life is not the exclusive property of any one person; it is linked to so many other lives as in a web.

Some of the illuminating moments in the novel occur in close proximity to the perennial rhythms or seasonal cycles of nature in which we may encounter a vast simplicity. While Sandip's philosophy is that of violent exploitation of nature—the aggressive ego at work—Nikhilesh's attitude is one of heightened and alert passivity, which learns not to submit nature to any violent moulding. In his fourth monologue, Nikhilesh's moment of clarity about Bimala takes him out of the broken cage of their bedroom into the ample light of an autumn afternoon. There, amidst the agitated twitter of birds and the profusion of flowers he notices a bullock cart with two unyoked bullocks. One is grazing and the other basking in the sun, its eyes closing in comfort as a crow pecks away at the worms on its body. Nikhilesh feels the intimate heartbeat of all that is simple yet vast in the universe, its warm breath mingled with the fragrance of flowers seems to fall on him. At that moment of oneness with nature, he understands the simple duty that lies before him when his thought turns to Panchu, trapped in poverty and exploitation, lying like that bullock in the autumn sun on the entire expanse of Bengal, eyes closed not in comfort but in fatigue, disease, and starvation. He can also see Panchu's fat and pious zamindar, Harish Kundu, who reminds him of the oily green scum on the putrefied waters of a stagnant pond sending off poisonous bubbles from time to time. In one moment the simple truth clarifies his vision and moves him away from idle introspection, endless debate and uncertainty to activity directed surely towards a clear and realisable goal. Thus, in moving out of the architecture of companionate domesticity (the bedroom) into the open, in moving from inside to outside, from self-absorption to solidarity with the vast stream of life, Nikhilesh dynamically links the home and the world.

Notes

1. Bimala's first monologue, *Rabindra Rachanabali*, vol. 4, Vishwabharati, 1987, 474. All references are to this edition. The translations are all mine. References have not been made to the Macmillan English translations not only because the translation is unsatisfactory, but also because entire passages and sections are omitted without explanation. The passage quoted above, for instance, has been omitted.

WORLD/*BAIRE*

7

Contesting Modernities: The Two Men in *Ghare Baire*

SHARMILA PURKAYASTHA

In an essay in the well-known *Sabuj Patra,* Tagore responded to the controversy surrounding the novel, *The Home and The World,* by stating that, the "spirit of the modern age had influenced the author...but the influence belongs to the purely artistic plane... [the writer] is concerned only with art, and if the reader chooses to invest him with some other concerns, it is really the reader's own and the writer should not be saddled with its responsibility."[1] The "spirit of the modern age" is where this

Svati Joshi and Kumkum Sangari read the first draft of this article. I thank them for their suggestions and comments.

essay begins. The attempt is not to define modernity as it prevailed in early twentieth-century Bengal or to explore the issue of derivation or innovation, which is far beyond the scope of this paper, but to examine the textual responses to contesting forms of modernity centering on the issues of nation and gender in the context of swadeshi Bengal.

Nikhilesh and Sandip, the two young men in Tagore's *The Home and The World,* represent modernity not as an unequivocal monolith but as a contested terrain. Their definitions of nation and womanhood are contradictory and inconclusive as is manifested in their tragic clash over Bimala's and in the nascent nation's identity, particularly evident in the issue of boycott of foreign goods. It is significant that the conflict is not framed in the usual discourses of youth and age or past and present. Both contestants are young, energetic, and romantic men of newly awakened Bengal. Yet, their visions of the future, of themselves, of their relationships, are entirely different and the "home" and "world" get scripted differently in this clash where two kinds of masculinities (reformist and revolutionary), and two notions of political freedom (self-development and boycott) are posed. This difference has deep implications for Bimala, the third young protagonist of the novel.

How and why did Tagore insert two young and modern men who are both rivals and friends within this debate over modernity? And how does one understand modernity from within a quiet and traditional[2] feudal world and, equally, that which emerges from political turbulence? Early on in the text, Sandip uses the adjective "amphibious" to describe the double nature of Nikhilesh's living room, "half women's apartment, half men's".[3] Like the living room, the realm of the personal in the novel is porous, as it absorbs ideas and opinions from the world outside. Tagore's novel too is amphibious creating many porous sites of contradictions and contests. This essay seeks to understand the processes that went behind some of these porous sites of contradictions in the construction of modernities; the social and economic wherewithal which made these two men so distinct, different, and yet similar.

It is divided into two parts: the first part outlines the problematic and maps the contours of bhadralok modernity both within the historical context and in the text (which reveal the affinities between the two men). The second part examines the differences between the two men and the political significance thereof.

I

Opposites or Doppelganger?

The historical context of the novel, the swadeshi period in Bengal (1903–08), is "extremely rich [in] ideological controversies".[4] Some of these find their resonance in the novel through the debates over swadeshi between Nikhilesh and his friend, Sandip. The two men are presented as opposites with contrary views on just about everything from nation building to matters of philosophy, art, sexuality, and history. What's more, their disagreement spills over into their personal thoughts and actions. Since the novel is set in the turbulent times of Swadeshi Andolan, the two men represent the oppositional views of autonomous self-development, and it is shaped out of views that Tagore himself propagated and militant Hinduism that the extremists believed in (minus the terrorist agenda).

The complicating issue in this otherwise straightforward story of worthy and unworthiness is a small but significant detail: the fact that both men share something in common. In the poetic language of Nikhilesh's teacher, this sharing is explained as, "I now see that though you two do not rhyme, your rhythm is the same", or as he says a little before this, "his [Sandip's] religion is of the obverse side of truth, like the dark moon, which is still a moon for all that its light has gone over to the wrong side" (106). The German word that comes closest to describing this phenomenon is doppelganger, which means a "double walker" or a ghostly counterpart of a living person; a negative alter ego. Obviously, Sandip is no "ghostly presence" in the text, as he is only too real, but the relationship between the two men is not merely oppositional.

A closer look at the text reveals the commonality that both men share: they are college friends who bonded together over club discussions on translations of Browning. Both of them are young and energetic and have dreams of the future. They are aware of the importance of history and believe that the past is important in understanding the present. Both of them go off to unknown destinations at the end of the novel, and even though it is shown that Nikhilesh is wounded, it is not clear whether he will live or die. And, most importantly, both of them are engaged in defining the "new woman"; the woman of the future.

Why does Tagore insert this aspect of doppelganger into the text? Why must Nikhilesh share anything in common with a man whose only maxim is "I want"? There can, arguably, be two related reasons why Tagore presented the theme of doppelganger: one to make Bimala's attraction for Sandip credible (for, if revolutionary ardour is premised on personal male unworthiness, then female desire is also compromised and Bimala is attracted to Sandip in no uncertain terms); secondly, to show that what bonded the two men was not just their gender but also their class. It is in this context that he created a more credible story of two alternating and contesting modernities presented by two similar yet dissimilar characters. While the theme of doppelganger recognises the shared similarity, it does not form a significant part of the novel as the narrative strategies in the rest of the novel do everything to dispel or reduce it to moral comparisons.

A reading against the moral grain of the novel, then, is a necessity for a more enabling comparison between the two men. And since the novel is set against the backdrop of the swadeshi movement, the tendency to look for actual historical figures for the characters or the other tendency to treat the novel as an authentic social and political document is fraught with problems. Nikhilesh and Sandip cannot be exchanged for "real" people or explained away as tools of authorial intention. As characters they inhabit an aesthetic domain and are endowed with individuality and autonomy. But, since imaginative writing doesn't happen in a vacuum, the connections between character and history are necessarily complex. Tagore wrote well after the turbulence of the Swadeshi Andolan had died down, and the "historical" nature of the story is an imaginative reconstruction of possible events or episodes. The fictional space is the imaginative terrain where narrative and history coalesce and ideologically shape characters and their histories. The question, then, is not whether Sandip or Nikhilesh are based on real historical personages, but how and why Tagore ideologically locates his characters within the times. It is no doubt possible to read Nikhilesh as an ideal exceptional hero created in troubled times by an exceptionally gifted artist. But it is equally necessary to examine what draws him to Sandip, what removes him from Bimala's politicisation, what withholds him from engaging in direct politics of confrontation either at home or outside. Equally, it is important to delve beneath and behind the moral story of the grasping and unscrupulous Sandip and uncover the story of upward mobility of a discontented and educated youth in troubled times.

Education and Social Class

The economic difference between Nikhilesh and Sandip and the fact that Nikhilesh had supported Sandip earlier is mentioned more than once. This information is important as it establishes Nikhilesh as Sandip's benefactor, while at the same time it confirms Sandip's lowly status and money-grubbing ways. Sandip's background is made not only unimportant but irrelevant since the linearity of the events in the text makes his arrival in Nikhilesh's home coterminus with the advent of Swadeshi Andolan (although he claims to have been a member of the Congress Party). Are these textual strategies deployed so as to make the reader recognise the caricature of the extremist leader without giving importance to circumstances? Tagore's curious reticence over Sandip's personal history is not without significance: the gaps and silences assert his lack of moorings which, in turn, affirm his predatory and wandering ways.

Where and how would one place Nikhilesh and Sandip in terms of social class? Nikhilesh is introduced as a zamindar whose unbroken ancestry goes back to Mughal times, and Bimala's first narrative introduces us to his lavish household with its multitude of retainers and extensive landed wealth. Unlike his older brothers, Nikhilesh is the first to acquire education and go to Calcutta for higher studies. He owns a house in the city and his rural estate of Sukhsar is an enormous one. We are told that the estate had seen the flux of fortunes as it jostled between the rent receiver and family.[5] However, in Nikhilesh's time, the estate is large enough to include the biggest trade centres in the district, large enough to host a great annual fair where thousands of pilgrims assemble, it had sufficient land and wealth to support a school and Nikhilesh's various failed swadeshi enterprises including a bank. The government's revenue from Nikhilesh's estate alone is seven and a half thousand rupees. Like others of his class, Nikhilesh doesn't need to use his education to earn his living; he lives off his land.

Sandip, on the other hand, is a rootless pauper. We are given no information about his background or family fortunes. Bimala's first narrative tells us how her husband supported his friend on a monthly basis and helped him in all his swadeshi enterprises. Before meeting him, Bimala is critical of him, for she feels that he has "*babu*" affectations and hardly looks like an ascetic or a poor man (in his photograph). Sandip also doesn't earn his living; his job, in the text, is to mobilise the rural youth to the swadeshi cause.

How does one locate an English-educated urban youth who has no means? How does one understand Sandip's social origins without taking recourse to moral categories which the novel constantly invites one to? Through the nineteenth century, a number of people migrated to the city in search of employment. Unlike the landless peasant or the poor cultivator, the bulk of persons who migrated were those who had some small petty landholdings in their villages and who moved to the cities in search of *kerani*/clerical jobs. Needless to say, this section also comprised the upper castes, as their social power in the village would enable them to avail of the new city opportunities. The census figures of 1891 show that "one-third of the shopkeepers, a tenth of the schoolteachers, one-fourth of the doctors, pleaders and lawyers and one sixth of the clerks had 'some interest in land, generally as intermediate tenants'."[6] Thus, caste status, connections with land, and also genteel poverty characterised the social and class origins of the intelligentsia of the late nineteenth century. Consequently, this class was inclined towards nationalism not only because of its intellectual orientation, but also because of growing unemployment at about the same period. As Partha Chatterjee notes, "provincial politics in Bengal (in the late nineteenth century) came to be dominated by the class of small rentiers in land. The Indian Association was set up in 1876 to voice the interests of precisely this class, following the split in the British Indian Association which was thereafter exclusively dominated by the big zamindars."[7]

Returning to Tagore's text, one is struck by the omissions in Sandip's background. We, however, do know (primarily from the Bengali text) that he went to college, stayed in a hostel, had numerous girlfriends, and studied philosophy. In his interactions with Bimala, he displays knowledge of Western art and poetry and recalls the clubbing days in college. His urbane disposition, his babu affectations, and *nawabi* manner belie his actual financial status—that of a rootless pauper. Though we are not told his caste, we infer that he, like Nikhilesh, belongs to one of the upper castes, as he eats with Nikhilesh and his wife and that causes no recriminations from the other women in the house.

Therefore, do Sandip and Nikhilesh belong to the same class? If class is understood as gradational and differentiated on grounds of social occupation, then they are not alike, as there is little in common between a zamindar and a pauper. If class is treated as relational in which one class exploits the labour of the other, then too, they are not alike. Nikhilesh belongs to the feudal landlord class which extracts the surplus from tenants, but he is a tax-paying landlord, who pays a fixed sum of revenue to the colonial government (perhaps that is why he never takes any oppositional stand against the British). Sandip's class origins, on the other hand, are hazy and unclear. Speculatively, Sandip's anger against the British and his nationalist fervour would suggest that he belongs to a class that lost employment opportunities in spite of education. Clearly this class could not exploit the labour of another class as it did not own any means of production. But it did have power and means of another kind: the power of education and caste and social control and domination thereof. Their economic interest would also desire and demand a different politics of a nation than that of a secure, landed class. Often characterised as the middle class or bhadralok, this social section was heterogeneous enough to bring very diverse people within its fold. The importance of education along with other factors such as abstinence from manual labour, radical potential for change and heterodoxy as well as reverence for traditionalism were some of the obvious markers of the bhadralok.[8] Thus, common factors united economically heterogeneous people, and the consequent cultural identity was integral to the self-perception of the bhadralok. The emphasis on common cultural identity allowed for "multiple class character"[9] within the bhadralok section and very different kinds of people such as absentee landlords, deputy magistrates, and junior clerks and schoolteachers could all be bhadralok. But, if, education was a means to an end (employment within the colonial apparatus), then it also simultaneously underlined the importance of money. This was certainly the case in higher education where high fees restricted the entry of lower castes and economically deprived sections. To give just one example: when Hindu College was re-established as Presidency College in 1855, the fee was raised from Rs 5 to Rs 10.[10] Thus, higher education was not only a means of social domination for the creamy layer within the bhadralok class; it was a powerful means of upward mobility for the same section within the colonial apparatus.

Modernity: Contradictions and Consensus

Nikhilesh and Sandip are from a common cultural class of the bhadralok, and their pursuit of education is a very important factor in understanding this shared background. Clearly, the difference in their social rank and financial status is subsumed under the common identity of bhadralok. Both of them are products of new education and social reforms and thus participate in a new and shared modernity. Both of them are deeply interested in the question of Bimala's womanhood and in the destiny of the country in keeping with the contemporary bhadralok preoccupation with nationalism and gender. Considered within this rubric of bhadralok identity, the affinities and differences between the two men can be placed within a more enabling axis of modernity rather than morality and modernity premised on a common cultural class.

Given that the bhadralok identity was premised on internal differences of rank, class origins, and occupation, the nature of modernity was not necessarily cohesive or homogenous, but marked by contradictions and contestations. The multiple-class character of the bhadralok allowed for ideological differences without open conflicts of interests. But consensus was needed for the project of bhadralok modernity to hold the internal differences in ideas and attitudes. The larger consensus on issues of religion, caste, and rejection of manual labour ensured a common class reaction to matters related to social and economic conflicts. In fact, throughout this period, bhadralok meant both upper caste and Hindu. While this exclusive identity based on caste explains the social relations and aspirations of only upper castes, the religious identity is not accidental. Obviously there were educated Muslims and rich landed families at that but, as the historian Rafiuddin Ahmed says, the relative absence of Muslims from higher education, the consequences of the Permanent Settlement on upper-class Muslim families, the question of identity and "backwardness", hindered the growth of a similar section of bhadraloks within the Muslim community.[11]

Tagore's text maps the contradiction and consensus between the two men within this discourse of modernity. Since both of them belong to a common cultural class, the contradictions can be understood as differences within a shared understanding of modernity. For instance, Sandip tries to sexually attract Bimala by educating her on Western art and poetry, while Nikhilesh builds on his conjugality by teaching his wife the finer points of political economy. Nikhilesh desire to dress his wife in the latest fashions and take her out of purdah is an obvious sign of his interest in matters of femininity, while Sandip's insistence on Bimala "discovering" herself is likewise a different notion of female subjectivity. Their views on nation are also striking: while one believes in an anti-imperialist model of nation, the other is concerned with internal fragmentation within the same model. The point is not whether what Nikhilesh believes in is better than what Sandip does (as it returns us to a simplistic, moral reading), but that the new notions that both men have on nation, family, female subjectivity, sexuality, and education are different ideological spaces within a common experience of modernity.

But, where consensus is derived from caste and religion, certain traditional attitudes are also preserved in this journey to modernity. Sandip's open worship of a Hindu past is obvious, yet, Nikhilesh's vocal rejection of Sandip's model of Hindu glory against his own model of India which believes in a secular identity does not have any vision for changing the conditions of Mirjan, the poor Muslim boatman who is harassed and whose livelihood is destroyed by Sandip and his followers. Moreover, neither Sandip nor Nikhilesh have any constructive programme for the Panchus of the world.[12] Between Nikhilesh's omissions and Sandip's commission, the shared attitudes on questions of caste and religion rest, and rest uneasily.

Besides caste and religion, another arena of contestation and consensus in the novel is that of gender. Modernity offers the greatest spaces to women, and both the men show new ideas of womanhood: conjugal equality and sexual emancipation. But, what the text also captures is the way in which patriarchies[13] insert themselves within new modernities to create new inequalities and new confusions. Nikhilesh as emancipated husband and head of household brings welcome changes, but his authority is not undermined as the male householder. The fact that Bimala cannot take financial decisions and has to stoop to steal money indicate that new ideas of womanhood do not take into account the question of female independence. Equally, Sandip's assertion of sexual emancipation gives Bimala a new identity as a woman. She herself notes in chapter three how she is consulted by Sandip on matters related to politics. However, this new world is controlled and ruled by men like Sandip, and Bimala has to be content being behind Sandip Babu and speak the voice of "common sense".

Caste, religion, and gender, then, define the matrix for bhadralok outlook and help in holding contradictions without threatening the entire experience of modernity. But differences in social rank and opportunities are real and equally important in understanding why the two men cannot share a common social and political future; their journeys are different and they cannot quite agree on mutual sharing.

II

The New Scion

Nikhilesh's journey from youth to maturity takes place in a society that undergoes rapid shifts and political upheavals. Even the society at the start of Nikhilesh's journey is neither static nor stable. Decadent aristocracy is contrasted with the new world of enlightenment, learning, and reforms. New definitions of conjugal happiness are ushered in, touching the lives of those women who have access to this world through men and marriage. Nikhilesh is set at the centre of this world as the new hero whose youth and yearning creates novel experiences and new structures of feelings. His definition of happiness is based on respect and equality, a feeling that the traditional Bimala doesn't quite adjust to. He wants Bimala to share his world fully and completely and therefore even suggests that both of them should go away to Calcutta after his grandmother dies. His new world is created in the bedroom and it is here in the dressing table, cupboard, and books that the new experiences find concrete shape. His self-reflexivity gives him a consciousness and concern for female oppression and is intimately connected with this world of new reforms. In this world, Nikhilesh can adorn his wife with the latest fashions, teach her political economy, take her out of purdah, experiment with his eccentric ideas of swadeshi, and also care for and support his widowed sister-in-law.

Nikhilesh can synthesise the demands of individuality with socialisation and creates a modern world based on the culture of reformist landed aristocracy that retains traditional family relations, respects natural inequalities, but does not risk open conflicts.[14] Social cohesion is very important to Nikhilesh's identity, notwithstanding his modernity. Loyalty, the best of feudal sentiments, is articulated through small incidents, such as when Panchu, a poor and oppressed tenant of a neigbouring zamindar, is afflicted by his conscience and comes to return a bunch of coconuts that he had stolen from Nikhilesh's garden because of his poverty.

In spite of his new definitions of conjugality, Nikhilesh doesn't break the old custom of social separation of husband and wife during the day. His new world of ideas is *dependent* on the continuity of traditional relationships, and his relations with both his master and his older widowed sister-in-law are important in this regard. With his sister-in-law, Nikhilesh enjoys a very affectionate relation because he was her playmate when she came as a child bride of nine years, and they grew up together. More importantly, as head of the household after his brother's death, the sister-in-law is dependent on him, and he indulges all her whims much to Bimala's chagrin. The importance that Nikhilesh gives to this traditional relationship can be gauged by his reactions to the "discovery" of his sister-in-law's decision to accompany them to Calcutta. The putative reason that the Senior Rani gives is that she can't bear to die alone, but Nikhilesh knows that "a true relationship [had] grown up between us, from our childhood up till now, and its branching foliage has spread and broadened over every room and verandah and terrace of this great house" (chapter twelve). With his teacher, Nikhilesh enjoys a very special relationship. He is the traditional tutor, mentor, and guardian who saves him from actually engaging with Panchu's miseries, intervenes on his behalf with Sandip's followers (who incidentally studied free in Nikhilesh's school and had subsequently turned swadeshi), and understands Nikhilesh's real pain at his marital separation.

Both marital happiness and social cohesion are disrupted by the swadeshi events. Confronted with the suddenness of swadeshi violence, Nikhilesh reaches the limits of his social identities of newly reformed husband and benevolent zamindar. For him, things *do* fall apart and the centre cannot really hold. The painful rupture in his life forces him to experience newer feelings of estrangement and existential angst. But neither can he break his social ties nor act repressively with his wife. Since he cannot envisage "open conflict", he retreats; chooses personal freedom over marital happiness, experiences loneliness and jealousy, and gets high-minded in refusing others. He refuses, for instance, to buy shares in the swadeshi cotton mill and justifies it on the grounds that he will not be party to the exploitation of the poor. He declines to comply with Bimala's demand for removing foreign goods from the local market and argues that it will affect the poor peasants and petty traders. The first refusal doesn't make any sense as he himself had wasted a lot of money in trying to set up swadeshi ventures, all of which had failed. More importantly, his own revenues are derived from a well-established exploitative system: feudal rent expropriated from the poor peasantry. And as far as Bimala is concerned, Nikhilesh's refusal has as much to do with rejection as with not wanting to be a part of boycott politics.[15]

As the novel proceeds, Nikhilesh retreats *mentally* into a world of the past: a world of traditional family virtues and social harmony. Significantly, his valuation of his relationship with his sister-in-law becomes inversely dependent on his devaluation of Bimala's marital affection and, thus, at the end he says, "She [Bimala] also felt the Senior Rani's claim over me was not based merely on our social connection, but went much deeper; and she was jealous of these ties between us, reaching back to our childhood" (chapter twelve). Quite the opposite from where he started: a new man in a traditional society who brought welcome winds of change in his marital life. But, before the new ideas of reform and conjugal happiness can be assimilated, a still newer world of ardour and passion, both politically and sexually, unleashes itself catching Bimala in a maelstrom of newly awakened feelings and leaving Nikhilesh isolated and rejected as a man of the past.

It is no coincidence that Nikhilesh's modernity is directed towards educating his wife and in individually trying out extravagant experiments for "improving" the lives of his people. In educating his wife, he participates in the wider contemporary ideas of female reforms and yet leads a secluded life within his estate. His experiments which pre-date the Swadeshi Andolan are individual in venture and do not require mobilising energies outside his estate. Education and class come together insofar as the former makes apparent the need for changing women's lot, but the latter restricts the need to individual action. Of course, Nikhilesh's criticism of swadeshi politics is not necessarily the only class response as Tagore inserts other Hindu zamindars such as Harish Kundu and Chakrabarti who respond enthusiastically to the call of boycott. Historically, a number of zamindars did participate in the Swadeshi Andolan, and in 1907, Aurobindo Ghosh in his programme of passive resistance argued for the benefits of landlords in the andolan. However, the total number of zamindars who were active in the Swadeshi Andolan was far fewer than the bulk of youth who belonged to the discontented sections. Not surprisingly, when in 1910, the British government wanted to deport 53 suspects who had been convicted for their role in the andolan, only four were sons of zamindars. While the novel represents "zamindari" as a continuous and unchanged given state of hierarchy, it should also be remembered that the term zamindar did not have a fixed meaning from the Mughal times to the period of Swadeshi Andolan. Bitter contests over land rights and fragmentation of estates which accompanied the Permanent Settlement of 1793 as well as the sales of land to the merchant class created many anomalies within this term. It is itself a case to wonder how and why Nikhilesh's estate escapes all internal feuds and fragmentation, and remains an ancient aristocratic estate. The story of bankruptcy is hinted at but relegated to the margins of the grandmother's tale, and it does not disturb any of the social relations within the text. And, it is a fact that Nikhilesh's economic relation (as a tax-paying zamindar) with the British administration sets him apart from his own fellowmen, and he recognises this in his unpopularity with the local swadeshi populace, which suspects him of being a collaborator. It is perhaps possible that Tagore, in creating an exceptional hero, also creates an exceptional and nostalgic story of heritage and lineage unchanged in its transience from Mughal to British administration.

The New Charlatan

The changes brought in by the Swadeshi Andolan ushers in the new hero, Sandip. A new sensibility defines heroism based on principles of opportunity, enterprise, and individualism and, as a corollary, a chaotic world flaunts its nationalistic aspirations, class inequalities, and communal divides. Sandip, not Nikhilesh is the new hero of the swadeshi world, and his brilliant oratory, sensuality, and belief in the passion of cruelty clash with Nikhilesh's ideas of reformist conjugal happiness and democratic beliefs. This new world is characterised by restless energy and destructive outcomes. Unlike

Nikhilesh's story, Sandip's narratives have no particular telos; and his "character" is not particularly coherent. His ruminations are not studies in sustained self-reflexivity or personal quest; instead they disclose his "dark" nature based on bad faith, arrogance, and greed. He is self-contradictory in his desires and actions: he grabs money from Bimala and then returns her jewel casket; he desires Bimala but feels pangs of guilt; he initiates events that lead to Panchu's and Mirjan's misery, but is indifferent to the results. His "realisation" at the end is only temporary as the reader is left with the feeling that he will go elsewhere and do exactly what he did here. He is fascinating but destructive.

Restless and ambitious, Sandip is keenly aware of his impoverished situation and his oppositional energies destabilise the plot of happiness and social cohesion. Bimala's attraction to him renders Nikhilesh's project of new conjugal harmony as obsolete and insufficient to the needs of female sexuality. His very presence in the living room causes ripples in the andarmahal, as the Senior Rani takes to eavesdropping, the maids fight each other, and the trusted guard, Nanku, is assaulted when he attempts to stop Sandip from entering the living room. And when the other Hindu zamindars are won over by Sandip's cause, Nikhilesh's position as a benevolent zamindar is undermined and he is exposed to charges of collaboration and inaction.

Since he is at the epicentre of the swadeshi turbulence, Sandip's sense of himself is always bigger and wider. In chapter three, he arrogantly announces to the readers, "All is clear to me. The curtain flaps, and through it I can see the preparations for the catastrophe." A little later he declares that he "must see this [Bimala's journey into modernity] out to the end of the Fifth Act." His confidence in his ability to be the dramatist of Bimala's life is both ridiculous and terrifying. His claims of immortality are indeed ridiculous as they make him theatrical and "stagey". But, his words are prophetic and terrifying, as Bimala's catastrophe happens and it happens because of him.

Sandip besides offering sexual appeal based on Western art and poetry also appeals to Bimala by tempting her with promises of a new future. He is the man of the future and she must accompany him in this new journey. But his vision of the future actually takes him back to the past, to the world of gods, goddesses, and worship. This, disguising of the past as the future, is perhaps the most disturbing feature of his personality. He offers Bimala a new destiny but simultaneously freezes her into an icon of the mother goddess. He rekindles caste hierarchies, and even his understanding of the man-woman relationship is based on male aggression and female passivity. He, thus, impudently offers old wine in new bottles.

Sandip's relations with Amulya, his chosen disciple, are based on hierarchy and patronage. Sandip cannot believe in his values unless he is "followed", and he demands complete and utter submission from his followers. He pretends to be a charismatic leader, but actually his brand of nationalism is communal, his leadership is no better than demagogy, and his personal actions are unworthy. Nationalism for Sandip is a prospective avenue for upward mobility and one which he grasps eagerly. Active and direct politics give him an opportunity to exhibit his education and a chance to improve his material condition, and the consequent "softness" in him makes him suspect and coarse. Besides giving importance to the pleasures of the flesh, Sandip makes no attempt to hide his desire for a materially better life. He wants to live and travel in style, and his parasitic living even before the andolan is a proof of this. His commitment to politics is more an indication of bettering his situation than a sign of his determination to rid the country of its oppressors.

Tagore's presentation of Sandip makes clear that upward mobility through nationalist politics is necessarily a bad thing. Swadeshi politics is wrong because coarse men like Sandip believe in it and use it for personal profit. It is no coincidence that Sandip and not Amulya is presented as the leader of swadeshi, as the latter has idealist leanings and is disinterested in matters of private gain. Amulya's death only confirms the destructive nature of swadeshi politics, as it leads to the death of innocence and idealism. It is inevitable that Sandip's chosen disciples, Amulya and Bimala, see through his game and reject him. Towards the end of the novel, when Sandip shows a rare bit of conscience and returns Bimala's jewels, the damage is not undone. It is poetic justice that the charlatan stands exposed and is hounded by the same "*Mussalmans*" whom he had contemptuously rejected and oppressed.

Tagore's presentation of a damaging form of politics and destructive men is convincing, but certain questions remain. What is surprising is that Tagore resolutely refuses to give Sandip any substantive subjectivity beyond cheap visions of power, theatricality, and grandeur. What is disconcerting is the manner in which Tagore fuses his antipathy for the politics of extremism with his distrust of Western-oriented sexual modernity without acknowledging that the two need not be one and the same. The stark binary between innocent idealism and opportunism, the difference between Amulya and Sandip, is unsettling as it underscores the relation between a leader and his follower. Since Tagore offers no information about Sandip, his story of upward mobility has no logic, no rational explanation and no coherence, other than opportunism. It is ironic that neither Bimala nor Amulya rejects him for his political beliefs (of Hindu revivalism and communalism) but for his personal immoral actions.

But could Tagore have written about the swadeshi times without including a restless hero, a discontented bourgeois youth who saw dreams and possibilities in troubled times? Unlike a historian, Tagore decides to tell a story, almost a decade after the upheavals had died down, and he tells it from a position of reformist landed wealth, which did not envisage "open conflicts". Thus, the theme of upward mobility is necessarily morally judged, and the presentation of Sandip is therefore, biased. But Tagore did diagnose a particular symptom of the new times: restlessness characterised by a new impudence in thought and boldness in action, which Nikhilesh and his world cannot expel or deal with. In another context, of European revolutions of the nineteenth century, Franco Moretti says that charlatanry is not just a moral problem that revolutions throw up but "without 'a certain amount' of it, revolutions would be impossible. More than a degeneration of revolution, charlatanry seems to be the disturbing presence. Disturbing, yet reasonable, for only the 'impudence' of thinking themselves better than they are can give the protagonists' destructive thrust that *symbolic legitimacy* which their 'reality' never could."[16] True, the Swadeshi Andolan was no revolution and Sandip hardly gives any "symbolic legitimacy" to the theme of extremist politics in nationalism; but the andolan was a very important historical event which gripped Bengal. For Tagore, the failure of the Swadeshi Andolan characteristically offered a justification for the repudiation of this new attitude.[17]

Notes

1. *Sabuj Patra, Agrahayan,* 1322. Qtd. in Niharranjan Ray, *An Artist in Life: A Commentary on the Life and Works of Rabindranath Tagore,* Trivandrum, Univ. of Kerala Press, 1967.
2. It should be clarified that the word, "traditional" is not being used here as revivalism but in its more obvious sense, that is, that which has been in existence for long.
3. "Sandip's Story", chapter 3, 52, *The Home and The World,* trans. by Surendranath Tagore, London, Penguin 1985, New Delhi, Penguin, 1999. Unless otherwise indicated, all references are taken from this Indian edition of the English translation.
4. Sumit Sarkar, *The Swadeshi Movement in Bengal,* 31.
5. In colonial times, the government collected taxes from the landlord who extracted rent from the tenants. If the landlord failed to pay the tax because of debt, the court could attach the property and even sell it. In the text, the term "receiver" is used to designate the court official.
6. Quoted in Tithi Bhattacharya, *The Sentinels of Culture: Class, Education and the Colonial Intellectual in Bengal (1848–85),* New Delhi, OUP, 2005, 56.
7. Partha Chatterjee, *Bengal 1920–47: The Land Question,* Calcutta, KP Bagchi, 1984, 12–13.
8. Pradip Sinha, "Social Change" in *History of Bengal (1757–1905),* ed., N. K Sinha, Calcutta, University of Calcutta, 1967. Also Pradip Sinha, *19th Century Bengal,* 1965, and Rajshekhar Basu, "The *Abhijat* and the Urban Ambience" in Ranjit Kumar Ray, ed., *Retrieving Bengal's Past: Society and Culture in 19th and 20th Century,* Calcutta, Rabindra Bharati Univ. Press, 1995. Sinha also points out that within a traditional society with very little structural change, the filtering down of the "*Bhadralok* mentality" into both the mercantile section as well as the higher artisan class produced a sheer heterogeneity

which made it impossible to acquire a class character, unlike the Western middle class.

9. This concept is taken from Eric Olin Wright's *Classes,* London, Verso, 1985, in his analysis of "Contradictory Class Locations". While mapping the "middle class", Wright says, "Instead of regarding all positions as located uniquely within particular classes and thus as having a coherent class character in their own right, we should see some positions as possibly having a multiple class character; they may be in more than one class simultaneously" (43). Although, Wright's work is within the Western capitalist system, this concept is helpful in understanding the "multiple class character" of the bhadraloks in Bengal.
10. Bhattacharya 15.
11. See Rafiuddin Ahmed, *The Bengal Muslims (1871–1906): A Quest for Identity,* Delhi, OUP, 1981.
12. Historians have noted the inherent class character of the swadeshi movement wherein rich zamindars and educated but unemployed youth (naturally upper caste) joined hands, and the mass of the agrarian or urban poor were not sufficiently mobilised to participate in the struggle for freedom. Also, the failure to include either the rich Muslim landlords or the poor peasants reveals the communal nature of the movement, and the riots of 1907 are themselves a product of this politics. See Sumit Sarkar, *The Swadeshi Andolan* and Hiren Chakrabarti, *Political Protest in Bengal: Boycott and Terrorism (1905–1918),* Calcutta, Papyrus, 1992.
13. The preference for plural, "patriarchies", instead of the singular, "patriarchy" in the essay is taken from the Introduction to Kumkum Sangari and Sudesh Vaid, eds., *Recasting Women: Essays in Colonial History,* Kali for Women, 1989. In fact, the Introduction is very useful in understanding why there cannot be a one-to-one relation between class and patriarchies as the latter have a "relative autonomy and a different duration" (5).
14. See Franco Moretti, *Way of the World: The Bildungsroman in European Culture,* London, Verso, 1987. In chapter one, Moretti, points out the aristocratic nature of the classical *Bildungsroman.* According to him, such texts convince the bourgeois reader of the social cohesion of the aristocratic universe as opposed to the cultural confusions attendant on the bourgeois notions of individual autonomy.
15. It has been suggested that Nikhilesh's situation as the "husband betrayed" is a novel one and that he suffers "*viraha*", on account

of his love for Bimala. Equally, it has been suggested that Nikhilesh represents an "alternative masculinity", which is simultaneously premised on the "inadequacy" of nineteenth-century male reforms. Firstly, Nikhilesh's "viraha" a form of feminising, is extremely doubtful, because what he experiences is hardly what Bimala thinks or feels; either at the start of his journey or at the end when he retreats into what is recognisably a male bastion, asceticism. The argument that Tagore affirms in Nikhilesh, the very best of nineteenth-century male reforms, is a persuasive one but where and how does one understand the "inadequacy"? Instead, of looking at the problem as a problem of masculinity, per se, it would be worthwhile to examine the limits of reformist landed ideology which would naturally be male. See essays by Tanika Sarkar and Sumit Sarkar in P. K. Datta, ed., *Rabindranath Tagore's Home and the World: A Critical Companion,* New Delhi, Permanent Black, 2003.

16. Moretti 109.
17. Recent criticism has recognised how, through Sandip's portrayal, the text is able to communicate meaningfully to a contemporary post-independence audience, which has and is witnessing the reactionary agenda of Hindu nationalism. Undoubtedly, Tagore's understanding of the fragility of the secular fabric during the swadeshi era is remarkable, and he is able to translate the same in this novel. However, it must be remembered that sectarianism was neither then nor now the only real threat to modern India. The fact that Tagore refuses any idealist and revolutionary hopes in Sandip is perhaps a very strong reason why this novel remains staunchly bourgeois in its appeal and aspirations.

8

The Peasant in *Ghare Baire*

SUMANTA BANERJEE

I

Hovering behind the scenes of the emotional and political tensions within the Nikhilesh-Bimala-Sandip triangle is the Bengal peasantry. Distant echoes of the Permanent Settlement, the zamindar-peasant relationship, and the Hindu-Muslim conflict in rural Bengal keep reverberating through Rabindranath's narrative. *Ghare Baire/ The Home and The World* ends with an ambiguous reference to these tensions—the readers not knowing who kills Amulya, whether Nikhilesh is dead or whether he will survive.

In a certain sense, this ambiguity reflects the ambivalence that marked the mentality of the late nineteenth- to early twentieth-century Western-educated, liberal-minded, reformist Bengali bhadralok zamindars in their perception about—and relationship with—the complex reality of Bengali peasant life. They were descendants of the absentee landlords who were products of the 1793 Permanent Settlement that allowed them to continue to collect rents, often at exorbitant rates, from tenants who worked on their lands. Yet, some among them, either instructed in the values of bourgeois liberal humanism in educational institutions like Hindu College of Calcutta or having been personally exposed to the sufferings of their tenants and peasants in their estates, felt guilty and sought to alleviate the lot of these poor people. Nikhilesh in *The Home and The World* is a typical representative of this group.

So was Rabindranath. Let us remember in this connection that Rabindranath was a zamindar owning large estates in eastern Bengal (Bangladesh today), which he inherited from his ancestors. It is necessary to comprehend Rabindranath's understanding of the Bengal peasantry, his attitude towards them, and his plans to improve their lot, before we enter into any discussion on his treatment of the peasant in *The Home and The World*. All through his life, he felt an enormous sense of guilt in his dealings with his tenants and labourers in his estates. After visiting the Soviet Union in 1930, where he observed the land reforms that had emancipated the peasants there, he wrote to his son Rathindranath Tagore about the Bengali zamindari system:

> … Mentally, I had always hated it. Today that feeling is more entrenched in my mind… I therefore feel ashamed of carrying on this business of *zamindari*. My mind today has come down from the pedestal of the upper strata to sit at the lower. My only regret is that I had grown up from my childhood as a parasite…"[1]

It was during his youth, in the late 1890s, when Rabindranath used to visit his estates to supervise the collection of rents from his tenants, that he became sensitised to the sufferings of the poor and landless peasants who often came to meet him and tell him their woes. He drew upon this experience to write some of the most moving short stories about the socio-economic reality of Bengali rural society. He became acutely aware of the abject economic poverty and social oppression that his *prajas* (tenants and peasants) were undergoing, thanks to an agrarian system over which he and his family were presiding.

Yet, he could not shake off his role as a feudal landlord, since, according to him, he needed the rent from his prajas to pay off debts incurred by his ancestors as a result of their extravagance. Much later, in a letter written to his daughter-in-law, Pratima Devi, in 1930, he narrated his dilemma at that time, speaking about his general disgust with the "profligacy of rich families", and wondering how soon he himself could put an end to his worries by paying off all his family debts and "stop once and for all future indebtedness."[2]

In the same letter, Rabindranath further expressed his sense of guilt at his failure to carry out his plans to reform the landlord-peasant relationship in his estates as a young zamindar. "We should not maintain ourselves at the expense of our poor peasant subjects," he wrote. "This is something which I had believed in for a long time. Since ages, I had hoped that our zamindari would become the zamindari of our subjects—and we would remain like trustees only. We would take a few necessary provisions like food and clothing—but as their partners. But I found that over the years, the chariot of zamindari didn't follow that path. Besides, when my debts went on increasing, I also had to remove such a plan from my mind. I felt sad at this, but didn't say anything…"[3]

It is an honest self-appraisal of the limitations that bound a bhadralok zamindar's reformist impulses and plans. It should be noted that Rabindranath, as a young reformist landlord in those days, did not think about the abolition of zamindari, but envisaged a more benevolent system of zamindari where the peasants would continue to work on the land of the zamindar, share the produce with him, while the zamindar would remain the trustee—the ultimate owner of the land, who would tell the peasant how he should behave, what he should plant, how much he should give his landlord, how he should educate himself. Rabindranath's genuine concern for his poor subjects was thus overlaid with an attitude of patriarchal patronisation that the liberal bhadralok zamindars nursed towards them. According to them, their peasants were not capable of self-development, and they therefore needed their landlords as trustees!

At the same time, Rabindranath appeared to understand the cynical response of the peasantry to such bhadralok reformist attempts—having observed the peasants in his estates from close quarters in a very perceptive manner. In a speech delivered at a meeting of a philanthropic organisation in Calcutta in 1915 (a year before his *Ghare Baire* came out), he narrated how he had enlisted the help of some young educated bhadraloks to work in villages to train the peasants in improving their health, education, and earning capacities—but had failed. Explaining the reasons, he said: "The educated people despise the uneducated from their gut level. It is difficult for them to mix with the villagers of the lower orders and behave towards them with proper respect and affection. We are bhadraloks, and we never forget that as bhadraloks we have the right to demand from the lower orders all that we require. We therefore expect that they will bow down to us immediately, accepting our arrival at their village to do good for them as a blessing for them, that they will obey whatever we ask them to follow. But what happens is just the opposite. The peasants of the villages do not trust the bhadraloks. From the very beginning, they regard the arrival of the bhadraloks as a nuisance, and suspect their motives as wicked. We cannot blame them. Because, they have not seen in their experiences people living at the top coming down without any personal interest to help those living at the bottom. On the contrary, it had been the other way round..."[4]

But having described acutely this attitude of the peasants towards the bhadraloks, Rabindranath attributes their suspicion to the lack of intelligence among the peasantry: "*Jader buddhi kam, tara buddhimanke bhoy korey*" (Those who are less intelligent, are fearful of the intelligent people).[5] Here again we find the same patronising assumption that identifies intelligence with those enjoying socio-economic power (that is, the educated zamindars in this case), and lack of intelligence with their subjects who are deprived of that power. Yet, such assumptions have been found to be totally unwarranted in the light of historical and socio-anthropological research that reveals that peasant intelligence is not only the reservoir of valuable ancient knowledge, but also judiciously adopts or rejects new ideas according to their needs. Just as illiteracy among the peasantry cannot be dismissed as ignorance, literacy among the educated need not be privileged as knowledge.

To come back to *The Home and The World*, Nikhilesh to a certain extent reflects the concerns, the anxieties, and the sense of guilt that Rabindranath himself suffered in his tensions between his zamindari obligations, on the one hand, and the sight of the sufferings of his tenants and the agricultural labourers working on his land, on the other. Nikhilesh also projects the reformist zeal of Rabindranath as a young zamindar trying to help these poor tenants and labourers to become self-reliant—albeit within and under the protection of the zamindari system.

Nikhilesh also represents another dimension of Rabindranath's political philosophy. He betrays the same ambivalence that tore Rabindranath's soul during the swadeshi movement in the first decade of the twentieth century following the announcement of the partition of Bengal in 1905. Rabindranath was torn between the passionate desire to be a part of the movement (expressed not only in the numerous patriotic songs that he composed during that period, but also by his active participation in street demonstrations) and by his revulsion of the methods used by the Hindu bhadralok political leaders of the swadeshi movement, that is, by both the acts of violence against the British rulers and non-violent methods such as boycott of British-made goods. The latter when it assumes violent forms becomes a major issue in a debate in *The Home and The World*. Nikhilesh, who lends support to the principle of swadeshi by encouraging and investing in indigenous cottage industrial enterprises—even at the risk of incurring heavy losses—protests against Sandip's forcible imposition of boycott of foreign-manufactured goods on the poor villagers, some of whom survive by selling them. Since Rabindranath wrote *Ghare Baire* in 1916—a whole decade after the tumultuous events of the swadeshi movement—he could be more dispassionate than he was during his involvement with the movement in those days, and looking back at the past, he could be more critical of the methods used by the swadeshi politicians.

It is through the mouth of Nikhilesh's teacher, Chandranath Babu, that Rabindranath voices his disappointment at the swadeshi movement's failure to build up a popular and viable base for the use of indigenously manufactured consumer goods. Despite all admiration for swadeshi efforts to manufacture such goods, the common consumers quite often found them inferior in quality and more expensive than the foreign goods. This was inevitable, given the superior technology of the foreign manufacturers, the mass production of their goods that allowed them to sell at cost-benefit rates, and their unrestricted import into India. It was indeed an unequal competition between swadeshi and foreign (mainly British) manufacturing concerns. As a result, even in those days of nationalistic euphoria, among consumers in the markets of Bengal, the preference for foreign goods prevailed over the patriotically inspired choice of indigenous manufactures.

Chandranath Babu brings out this ground reality in a debate with Sandip's young followers—middle-class students—when they come to Nikhilesh, demanding that he must banish foreign goods from his market in his estate in Sukhsar. He confronts them with a picture of the different slots in the network of rural-urban commerce, and reminds them how they had failed to ideologically convert these slots: "You want dealers, who have not taken your vow (to boycott foreign goods), to buy that yarn (swadeshi-manufactured); weavers, who have not taken your vow, to make it up; then their wares eventually to be foisted on to consumers who, also, have not taken your vow." Since the ideological initiation ("taking the vow"—the term used in the contemporary parlance of the swadeshi movement) has failed, the deficiency is being sought to be compensated by the swadeshi leaders and activists through coercion—by forcing some of the villagers to give up their trade (in buying and selling foreign goods) on which they survive. Chandranath Babu reminds these middle-class students of the plight that the poor villagers would face because of the coercion: "You are well-off, you need not mind the cost. The poor do not want to stand in your way, but you insist on their submitting to your compulsion. As it is, every moment of theirs is a life-and-death struggle for a bare living; you cannot even imagine the difference a few pice means to them..."

As for the problems of swadeshi production, Chandranath Babu gives us a good-humoured account of the failed attempts to manufacture cloth by his pupil, Nikhilesh. In a show of solidarity with the swadeshi movement, Nikhilesh had bought yarn from Indian mills and started a weaving school to get it woven. But Chandranath Babu, a sceptical and pragmatic old soul, sarcastically speculates about the fate of the neophyte Nikhilesh's endeavours : "...to judge by his past brilliant business exploits, by the time his cotton fabrics leave the loom their cost will be that of cloth-of-gold; so they will only find a use, perhaps, as curtains for his drawing room, even though their flimsiness may fail to screen him."

But under this debate over indigenous versus foreign manufactures, there lay hidden a more important agenda which had grave implications for the poor peasantry in Bengal during the swadeshi movement. It was the issue of hegemony over the rural poor. It was a tussle between competing socio-political forces in the contemporary Bengali countryside. Who would control the peasantry and how? In *The Home and The World*, Nikhilesh's arguments with Sandip and his interventions in support of his prajas, are expressions of this tussle.

We can discover shades of a conflict between the self-chosen patriarchal but benevolent norms of an educated Bengali liberal section of the zamindari class (which took upon itself the role of protecting the interests of their subjects) and the arrogant attitude of a new generation of middle-class political leaders who had intruded in rural society and were determined to establish their hegemony over the peasantry, with the help of the more feudal and oppressive section of the zamindari class.

Although friends, Nikhilesh represents the former and Sandip the latter. This conflict around the issue of hegemony over contemporary Bengali rural society forms the backdrop for Rabindranath's novel.

II

The peasant appears in *The Home and The World* later—when we are almost halfway through the narrative. He reveals himself—in the form of Panchu, the tenant of a zamindar who is Nikhilesh's neighbour. He comes to Nikhilesh one day with a basketful of coconuts. Nikhilesh suspects that Panchu is offering the coconuts because he needs money from him. But Panchu refuses the money offered by Nikhilesh and explains his act as one of repentance for having stolen some coconuts from Nikhilesh's garden earlier when he was hard pressed. Rabindranath here brings face to face two different minds—the bhadralok zamindar's mind which is suspicious, and yet generous towards the peasant, and the peasant mind, which is willing to cheat the zamindar when necessary, but eager to recompense him as soon as possible. How does one explain this paradox in the peasant mentality? Is this a continuation of a tradition where the peasant while recognising that the zamindar exploits him, displays a loyalty that is born of conventional socio-religious values and norms?

Nikhilesh then describes Panchu's life and poverty. He works from morning till night, making shell-bangles, bartering them and other knick-knacks for rice, and he barely manages to earn enough for two meals a day for his family during a little over half a year, their staple food being the "cheapest kind of seedy banana". From the description, Panchu appears to represent a typical peasant smallholder-cum-labourer of those days, who owned and worked on a tiny plot from which alone he could hardly feed his family all through the year. He was therefore compelled to labour as a tenant on a zamindar's land, which helped him to earn some wage in cash or kind, which meagre income again he had to supplement by selling odd and ends in neighbouring villagers. It was a precarious existence, endangered not only by seasonal uncertainties such as droughts and floods that affected agricultural production, economic factors such as fluctuations in the market price, and the ever-present threat of eviction by the zamindar but also by feudal norms of a rural society. The odds were heavily loaded against the poor peasant, especially if he came from the lower caste. This becomes explicit when we next meet Panchu. This is soon after his wife had died of lingering consumption. We learn that he had already sold part of his land and mortgaged the rest to meet the doctor's bill for his wife's treatment. Over and above this, he was now facing the socio-religious obligation of undergoing a "purification ceremony to cleanse himself of sin and to propitiate his community", which would cost him "one hundred and twenty-three rupees"—a large amount for a poor peasant in those days! Forced to submit to the dictates of the Brahmin priesthood in the village, he cries out: "...There is no escape from the offerings I have to make to the Brahmins." These offerings ranged from feasts for the Brahmin residents of the village on occasions like weddings and funerals, to frequent presents to the powerful among them to keep them in good humour. If he failed to carry out these obligations, the poor Hindu lower-caste peasant in rural Bengal in those days could have found it difficult to obtain social sanction and religious sanctification for the rites of passage in his family. If the Brahmin priest refused to sanctify them, the family would be considered an outcaste in the village. When Nikhilesh, highly indignant at such practices, advises Panchu not to submit to them, Panchu explains his dilemma in plain terms: "There is my eldest girl, sir, she will have to be married. And my poor wife's last rites have to be put through." Obviously, he cannot conduct either of the two rites of passage without the blessings of the Brahmin priest.

Nikhilesh's immediate response to Panchu's problems is always philanthropic—providing a "charity allowance" for Panchu, for instance. But Nikhilesh's teacher, Chandranath Babu, a far more pragmatic person who is also capable of looking beyond the present problem of an individual peasant, tells Nikhilesh that there are many more Panchus in the country, and his charity will not put an end to the lot of the peasantry in general. This awakens Nikhilesh to the realisation of the need to remove the "root of this sorrow in our country" (as he tells Bimala after his encounter with Panchu). But Bimala dismisses his concerns, since she believes that there is "a lower unit of measure for the trials and troubles of the 'lower classes'." In other words, according to her—like many other upper- and middle-class observers—the peasants have a high suffering threshold. So, what was unbearable pain to Nikhilesh and his reformist followers could be glossed over, in the contemporary common bhadralok parlance, as a common daily suffering that was borne stoically by the poor peasants. The middle-class argument ran like this—since they are used to bearing it, why should we interfere to make them aware of the option of a low-pain threshold?

Nikhilesh tries to rebel against this upper- and middle-class assumption. In his mental conflict with Bimala, he distances himself from her attitude towards the lower classes. In his introspection, he explains his position very clearly in these words (which unfortunately have been left out from the English translation): "I cannot push away those who are my subordinates to a far away corner, and dismiss them as an inferior species. My India is not an India of bhadraloks alone. I know it very clearly that the more my subordinates go down, the more India declines, the more they die, the more India dies." But Nikhilesh's lonely voice is drowned in the violence of the political upheaval that overtakes his estate soon after the partition of Bengal in 1905.

III

In 1905, Lord Curzon, the Viceroy, partitioned Bengal by carving out a new province of East Bengal and Assam. This had a major economic and communal impact on the Bengali-speaking population (both Hindus and Muslims) residing in these areas, and it led to political turmoil. Because of the religious composition of the population in the newly created province, the Bengali Hindus found themselves reduced to a minority among the Bengali-speaking people. Further, the Bengali Hindu zamindars and middle-class politicians all over Bengal felt threatened by a territorial split that would deprive them of their hitherto united clout in the state's politics. There are enough reasons to suspect that the British government, while citing administrative reasons for the partition, had the purpose of clipping the wings of the increasingly articulate Bengali Hindu political middle class first by dividing them spatially and secondly by propping up the majority Muslim community of the new province as their rivals.[6]

It may be noted that, at that time, Muslims in the agrarian sector of Bengal, in general, and in its eastern part, in particular, where they were in a majority, largely comprised peasants or tenants working on the lands of minority Hindu zamindars, while only a few Muslims were small landholders.[7] The Hindu zamindars, who were usually absentee landlords, lived in Calcutta, but administered their lands with the help of locally appointed Hindu *naibs* (managers) and *gomosthas* (rent-collectors), who also often took on the role of *mahajans* (moneylenders) extorting money from the poor peasants—both Hindu and Muslim. While, in an undivided Bengal, these zamindars and their agents as part of the Hindu majority could wield their power over the Muslim poor, in the new province, they felt threatened by the possibility of the majority Muslim community's (peasants, tenants, small landholders) getting together to challenge their authority. The East Bengal Hindu zamindars, therefore, found an ally in the Bengali urban upper- and middle-class leaders who launched the swadeshi movement against the partition of Bengal. Both the classes felt threatened by the partition—the former feared an outburst of reprisal by the hitherto oppressed Muslim peasantry, and the latter upset by the loss of its undisputed control over politics all over Bengal.

These political and economic fears of the Bengali Hindu upper and middle classes, rural gentry, and urban professionals converged with the widespread concern about the threat to the integrity of Bengali culture by the territorial partition of Bengal. Curzon's unpopular decision also revived the anti-British revolutionary sentiments that were lying dormant among the Bengali militant nationalists. Thus the swadeshi movement at the turn of the last century conflated a number of issues. It gave birth to a rich repertoire of patriotic songs, plays, and performances—much of which was contributed by Rabindranath, and whose songs composed during that period are still sung in both West Bengal and Bangladesh (the latter having adopted one of these songs as the national anthem). On the economic plane, as a show of protest against the colonial administration, the swadeshi leaders sought to assert their self-reliance by launching a campaign for setting up swadeshi or indigenous industries, encouraging the use of these swadeshi-manufactured goods among Bengali consumers, and, more importantly, the boycotting of all foreign goods. The swadeshi movement following the 1905 partition did indeed rouse a sense of militant nationalism among the Bengali youth, leading to innumerable revolutionary acts such as attacks on British officials and deeds of self-sacrifice. But we also have to note that some of the planks of the swadeshi campaign adversely affected sections of the rural poor—both Hindus and Muslims. The call for boycotting foreign goods was accompanied by the picketing of shops selling them, burning them in public bonfires, and forcibly stopping people from selling or buying them. The latter move in particular hit the rural poor who supplemented their meagre earnings from land by selling these goods in the local village markets after buying them from wholesalers.

In *The Home and The World*, the poor peasant, Panchu, becomes a victim of this swadeshi campaign against foreign-made goods. Significantly, Rabindranath situates Nikhilesh's zamindari in East Bengal which saw some of the most militant agitations as a part of the swadeshi movement in the 1905–07 period. Sukhsar, one of Nikhilesh's estates, is a major trade centre, and huge quantities of cotton yarn and woolen stuff are brought in by river transport for sale. Meanwhile, after a period of depression caused by financial constraints, Panchu is helped out by Nikhilesh's teacher, Chandranath Babu, who lends him money with which he buys imported cloth from the market and sells it in the villages. But soon, Sandip, the firebrand swadeshi leader, arrives on the scene and imposes an edict banning the sale and purchase of foreign goods. Nikhilesh's neighbour, the zamindar Harish Kundu, in whose land Panchu works as a tenant, becomes a great advocate of the swadeshi campaign to boycott foreign goods. He fines Panchu a hundred rupees for selling foreign cloth, and when Panchu pleads his inability to pay, he is beaten up and the entire bale of cloth is burnt to the shouts of patriotic slogans by Sandip and his followers. Harish Kundu further threatens to eject him from his ancestral holding thus putting an end to his tenancy. When Nikhilesh hears about it, he asks Panchu to lodge a complaint with the police. But Panchu says that no one in the village will dare to bear witness against the powerful zamindar Harish Kundu and his swadeshi supporters. Nikhilesh then proposes to buy up Panchu's holding and appoint him as his tenant, thus enabling him to continue his trading in cloth under his protection in defiance of Harish Kundu.

Panchu's reaction to this tussle between the two zamindars is typical of a helpless victim caught in a crossfire. He tells Nikhilesh: "...while you big folk are doing the fighting, the police and the law vultures will merrily gather round, and the crowd will enjoy the fun, but when it comes to getting killed, it will be the turn of only poor me." This is exactly what happens once Nikhilesh decides to buy Panchu's holding and appoint him as his tenant. In retaliation, Harish Kundu props up a false aunt to claim Panchu's holding and embroils him in a legal case. Both poor Panchu and his rich—but not worldly-wise—patron, Nikhilesh, would have remained bogged down for ages in a legal fight over Panchu's claim on his land, but for the intervention of Nikhilesh's guardian angel, his teacher, old Chandranath Babu. Always pragmatic, he comes to Panchu's rescue, by coming up with a shrewd stratagem to get rid of the aunt by paying her some money.

Nikhilesh's encounter with Panchu and his futile urgings to make him fight injustice as described in *The Home and The World*, are actually echoes of Rabindranath's own experiences in his role as an enlightened and reformist zamindar. He narrated one such experience in a speech which he delivered at a meeting in East Bengal during the height of the swadeshi movement. During one of his visits to the countryside to supervise his zamindari affairs, he came to know about a group of fishermen in the neighbourhood who were suffering immense hardship because of persecution by a senior police official. Rabindranath called the persecuted fishermen and asked them to file cases—either civil or criminal—against the oppressive police official and assured them that he himself would bring in a big lawyer from Calcutta to fight their cases. The fishermen folded their hands in supplication before Rabindranath and said to him: "Sir, what is the use of winning cases in law courts? If we stand against the police, we wont be able to stay even in our homes." Reminded of the vindictive power of the police (who even if defeated in the courts, could wreak vengeance on their victorious opponents by wielding their physical power and driving them out from their homes), Rabindranath observed: "I realized that the weak gets defeated even when he wins... The emaciated sick person dies under the burden of the expensive treatment." He then added that after this experience, he had always thought that "no gift was worth a gift; the only gift worth giving was power."[8] In other words, Rabindranath recognised that the gift of power—or what is termed as empowerment in today's political discourse—alone could help the poor and the weak to overcome oppression and exploitation.

But it throws up several questions that are relevant in the context of today's debate on the entire issue of empowerment of the poor. From the liberal humanist to the social democrat, from the Gandhian to the Maoist—everyone would agree that the economically poor and the socially underprivileged must gain power to improve their conditions and determine their future. The question is how this can be brought about. Should they struggle to capture that power from those who wield it now? What sort of pressures should they exert on the powerful? Or, should they wait for the latter to yield it to them as a "gift"? The term empowerment, which is in common use in modern political discourse, implies the giving of power to the poor and the weak by someone superior—either the state, or a voluntary organisation, or a more powerful agency (like the benevolent landlord as envisaged by Rabindranath in his days, or some philanthropic Western funding source as dreamt of today by the NGOs). It is a top-to-down process of power devolution. Political scientists and economists continue to debate whether such attempts at empowerment of the underprivileged by outside agencies, however well-meaning, really address their perceived needs at the ground level and make them self-reliant, or force them to become more dependent—both economically and morally—on these external sources.

But let us come back to *The Home and The World*. Although Panchu holds centre stage as the representative of the poor peasant in the novel, Rabindranath weaves in stories of other peasant families who suffer from worse forms of exploitation at the hands of their landlords. Thus, one of Sandip's devout followers tells Nikhilesh about another zamindar neighbour of his, one Chakravarti, who punished a recalcitrant tenant by setting the law on him till he was reduced to utter destitution. He narrates this incident, with a mixture of pity for the tenant and admiration for the zamindar's power: "When at last he was left with nothing to eat, he started out to sell his wife's silver ornaments, but no one dared buy them. Then Chakravarti's manager offered him five rupees for the lot. They were worth over thirty, but he had to accept or starve. After taking over the bundle from him the manager coolly said that those five rupees would be credited towards his rent." Another swadeshi follower of Sandip's tells Nikhilesh—again with the same mixture of revulsion and admiration towards the zamindar's methods—how a rent collector of Harish Kundu's treated a tenant who could not pay his rent: "...he was made to sell his young wife! Buyers were not wanting and the zamindar's demand was satisfied." The young swadeshi activist admits that the sight of that man's distress "prevented my getting sleep for nights together." But at the same time, he is full of admiration for the power that the zamindar wields over their tenants and agricultural labourers. While revolted by Harish Kundu's behaviour towards the poor tenant, he willy-nilly seems to accept it as a necessary evil. He appears to be more impressed by Kundu's control over rural society—the power that his swadeshi leaders need to harness in the Bengal countryside in their political campaign against the 1905 partition of Bengal. He tells Nikhilesh: "If anybody can save our country it is these Kundus and these Chakravartis and their officials."

This viewpoint of the middle-class swadeshi politicians and activists, who tended to ally themselves with authoritarian Hindu zamindars, was not a figment of Rabindranath's imagination. As is evident from contemporary data—both official and non-official—it was very much a part of the swadeshi movement, and, what is worse, it contributed a great deal to creating a communal divide between Hindus and Muslims in the rural society of East Bengal.

At this point, it is essential to discuss in brief the condition of the Muslim community in rural Bengal at the turn of the twentieth century. Although the Muslim characters do not feature prominently in *The Home and The World*, at the end of the novel, it is the intervention of the Muslims which decides the fate of its protagonists. We hear that they are looting Harish Kundu's treasury and attacking the women of his household. This immediately provokes Nikhilesh to ride to the spot to save the women—and this becomes his last journey. As mentioned earlier, the majority of the rural poor in

East Bengal were mainly Muslim small peasants, tenants, and agricultural labourers, who were employed by Hindu zamindars. They suffered both economic exploitation and social discrimination at the hands of these powerful landed interests. When they noticed that the swadeshi activists were aligning themselves with these zamindars, they quite understandably felt suspicious about the swadeshi agenda. Their suspicion turned into hostility when they saw the swadeshi politicians and activists increasingly adopting aggressive Hindu religious postures such as swearing by Goddess Kali, and, particularly, turning their ire against cow-slaughter. Although not widespread in Bengal, the practice of cow-slaughter was sometimes followed by Muslims as a ritual during religious festivals. This Muslim practice was picked up as a target of attack by the Hindu swadeshi activists, who upheld the orthodox Hindu religious belief that the cow was the mother of all Hindus. With the help of the Hindu zamindars, they therefore forcibly stopped Muslims from slaughtering cows. These overtly anti-Muslim gestures and acts by the swadeshi volunteers created an environment of hostility among the Muslim peasantry. This provided an ideal space for Muslim politicians aspiring for a popular base in Bengal to back up their claims for a separate constituency on a religious basis during negotiations with the British colonial administration. They enlisted the help of Muslim *mullahs,* who were sent to the villages to campaign against the swadeshi movement. With the support of Muslim small landowners and a rising Muslim middle class (who had been smarting from insults and humiliations heaped upon them for ages by the richer Hindu landlords), they rallied the Muslim peasants against the swadeshi movement, describing it as a Hindu-led assault on their religious rights. They urged the Muslim peasants to support the partition of Bengal, claiming that a separate East Bengal would enable the majority Muslims to get their own homeland, security of land, and jobs.[9]

Thus, the swadeshi campaign with an anti-Muslim bias often fuelled Hindu-Muslim tensions in several parts of East Bengal following the 1905 partition of Bengal. Sometimes, the religious confrontation revealed a class conflict, with Muslim peasants targeting oppressive Hindu zamindars. One such incident happened in Jamalpur in the Mymensingh district of East Bengal, during April-May 1907. Contemporary records indicate various reasons for the communal outbreak there. Jamalpur was famous for its cattle market, where mainly Muslim agriculturists gathered to buy cows and bulls. In 1907, taking advantage of the Hindu popular mood created by the anti-cow-slaughter campaign of the swadeshi activists, the local zamindar, who owned the market, increased the tax on the purchase of cows to an exorbitant rate. While he could have justified it in public as a disincentive to discourage Muslims from buying cows for slaughter, one also cannot escape the suspicion that he hoped to swell his coffers from the money extorted from these Muslims in the name of collecting tax. For this purpose, he not only relied on his hired goons but also enlisted the help of the police. Thus, when the Muslim peasants refused to pay the zamindar the enhanced tax, his goons and the police stopped them from taking the cows away. Violent clashes broke out. A section of the peasants raided the nearby *cutchery* office building of the zamindar of Gauripur and laid siege to it. They also looted the Dewangunj and Bakshigunj bazaars that were owned by the zamindar.[10]

Other reports, both official and non-official, suggest direct swadeshi provocation for the riots. They were apparently sparked off at a *mela* (fair) in Jamalpur on April 21, when Hindu swadeshi volunteers attacked Muslim shops that were selling foreign goods. The Muslim shopkeepers retaliated by attacking the volunteers. Soon riots spread to the northern part of the Jamalpur subdivision, and continued till May, 10.[11]

Although the Jamalpur disturbances were brought under control very soon by the colonial administration, the very fact that Muslim peasants could attack powerful Hindu zamindars aroused fears among the Hindu middle class in Mymensingh, who were used to looking upon their zamindars as their patrons and protectors. The incident became an important issue for the leaders of the swadeshi movement. They identified their anti-partition cause with the interests and fears of the Hindu zamindars and middle class of East Bengal. The head of the Jugantar group of the armed wing of the swadeshi movement at that time was Aurobindo Ghosh (who was very soon to leave revolutionary politics, and turn into a religious philosopher to be known as Sri Aurobindo of Pondicherry). He sent six of his emissaries, led by Bipinbihari Ganguly and Indranath Nandi, armed with bombs, revolvers, and pistols, to Mymensingh to protect the Hindus there.[12]

Significantly enough, the happenings in Mymensingh in 1907 caught Rabindranath's attention. He made several observations on the events at that time which reveal his views on Hindu-Muslim tensions as well as the zamindar-peasant conflict—the two issues often getting interlocked during the anti-partition movement. Referring to the behaviour of the swadeshi politicians in Mymensingh, he wrote in one of his articles: "Our orators became very angry when they failed to win the hearts of the Muslim peasants with their speeches in Mymensingh and other places. But it never occurred to them that at no time had we ever given any proof that we are genuine well-wishers of the Muslims, or the common people of our country. One should not therefore blame them if they suspect our pretensions to help them...."[13]

At around the same time, in 1907, addressing the Bengal Provincial Conference in Pabna in East Bengal, Rabindranath expressed his concerns about the on-going Hindu-Muslim riots and said: "We shall have to work much harder to stop this impending split among ourselves than we did with our utmost exertion to stop the division of Bengal."[14]

In another article written in the same year, he delved into the class dimension of the Hindu-Muslim conflict. In a bid to end the conflict on the national scale, he envisaged the creation of a *mahajati* or a larger nation that would discard sectarian prejudices. As for the rich-poor divide in the rural areas, he urged the youth to undertake constructive work in the villages to bridge the gap between the bhadralok and the masses.[15]

When after a decade, Rabindranath began writing *The Home and The World*, these concerns of his about the zamindar-peasant conflict and its convergence with Hindu-Muslim confrontation, obviously kept recurring in his mind. While locating the personal tragedy involved in the Nikhilesh-Bimala-Sandip triangle in the immediacy of the post-partition swadeshi movement, Rabindranath was also trying to re-examine his own views about the movement.

We therefore find him stressing the class relationship that ran as a subterranean stream beneath the swadeshi movement. The swadeshi revolutionary, Sandip, joins Harish Kundu, the zamindar, in organising celebrations to worship Goddess Durga, and Kundu extorts money from his tenants to cover the expenses. Meanwhile, a number of Muslim religious preachers arrive from Dhaka, who encourage the Muslims to kill cows. This annoys the Hindu villagers. Nikhilesh tries to intervene by reminding his Hindu tenants of animal sacrifice among Hindus too: "...those of us who are Shaktas go on with their animal sacrifices...We must in the same way, let the Mussulmans do as they think best. So please refrain from all disturbances." Nikhilesh is more assertive in his arguments with Sandip's followers when he takes a dig at the Hindu custom of sacrificing buffaloes to their goddess and dancing with their severed heads: "Buffaloes in this country ...give milk and are used for ploughing. And therefore, so long as we dance frantic dances on our temple pavements, smeared with their blood, their severed heads carried on our shoulders, religion will only laugh at us if we quarrel with Mussulmans in her name... If the cow alone is held sacred from slaughter, and not the buffalo, then that is bigotry, not religion."

But Nikhilesh's arguments and pleadings fall on deaf ears. Hindu and Muslim fanatic elements feed on each other to destroy Nikhilesh's estate Sukhsar. In the highly surcharged atmosphere, riots break out. In the last chapter, Rabindranath brings back to us Nikhilesh's teacher, Chandranath Babu, who arrives on the scene to give us the news: "...the Mussulmans are out of hand. They are looting Harish Kundu's treasury." He then adds (in an obvious reference to Harish Kundu's equally rapacious habits): "That does not so much matter." But to Chandranath Babu, "what is intolerable is the violence that is being done to the women of their house." It is this that provokes Nikhilesh to say: "I am off." The last sight we have of him is through Bimala's eyes—"galloping away on horseback with not a weapon in his hands" on his final journey. It almost evokes the romantic image of the Rajput warrior setting off to save the Hindu damsels from the clutches of the Mughal soldiers—without of course the "weapon", since Nikhilesh is committed to non-violence![16]

IV

The end of *The Home and The World* leaves us with a lot of questions. Who assaulted Nikhilesh? The "Mussalmans who had gone out of hand", or some swadeshi hotheaded fanatics whom Nikhilesh had antagonised by his opinions? Was he caught in a crossfire between the two groups while trying to prevent a clash? Such incidents of mediators being assaulted or killed in a battle of blind fury are not unknown. Who killed Amulya? Was the "bullet that went through his heart" fired by the police or by one of Sandip's devotees who considered Amulya a renegade deserving death. Such incidents also were not unknown in the history of the swadeshi revolutionary movement of those days. But Rabindranath refuses to provide any clue to the readers to help them come to a firm conclusion about these incidents that he describes in his novel. Was this ambiguity deliberate on his part—as a desperate attempt to nudge his Bengali readers to take up a position on their own, to question the ethics of the politicians and the mass politics which they had nurtured and which were determining social life in Bengal ?

Rabindranath's novel was published in 1916—a full decade after the violent tumult and political controversies of the swadeshi movement following the 1905 partition of Bengal. Why did he locate a story of an emotional triangle in a historical context situated a decade ago? After all, the partition was no longer an issue, since the British government had abrogated it in December 1911. Yet, Rabindranath meticulously represents the contemporary events and the public mood. Thus, while describing the looting of Harish Kundu's treasury and attacks on the women of his family by Muslims, it appears as if Rabindranath is actually borrowing from contemporary reports of the Mymensingh communal riots of 1907. These reports, appearing in Bengali Hindu-edited newspapers, highlighted incidents of Muslim attacks on Hindu properties, such as the plundering of the Gauripur Hindu zamindar's cutchery by Muslims, and they also circulated unconfirmed news about the violation of Hindu women by Muslims. Such rumours tended to reinforce the stereotype image of the Muslim male in the Hindu mind as a lecher suffering from uncontrolled lust for Hindu women![17]

Why did Rabindranath revive the memories of the 1905 swadeshi movement ten years later after its embers had died down? Or, did the embers really die down? Let us turn to the political and economic environment prevailing in Bengal when Rabindranath was writing the novel.

It may be recalled that the second decade of the twentieth century—the period during which Rabindranath thought of writing *Ghare Baire*—saw not only the continuation but also an aggravation, in certain respects, of the main socio-political trends that were set in motion during the anti-partition swadeshi movement of 1905. As we have noticed earlier from an analysis of his writings and observations during that period, Rabindranath was primarily concerned at that time with three problems: (i) how to reconcile his own understanding of the swadeshi cause (inclined more towards socio-economic reforms in the villages) with its militant version in the anti-partition movement (whose leaders and followers tended to assume a Bengali Hindu chauvinist character and often gravitated to the Hindu zamindar class—as evident in the 1907 Jamalpur riots); (ii) how to prevent Hindu-Muslim confrontations that often broke out as the class-based conflicts between Hindu zamindars and Muslim peasants; and, (iii) how to improve the conditions of the tenants and peasants by making them self-reliant and educating them in modern agricultural techniques.

These three questions, which occupied Rabindranath's thinking during the anti-partition movement in the first decade of the twentieth century, continued to haunt him even during the second decade. In fact, they were further fuelled by the events taking place around him. This period was marked by a number of major political developments. The First World War which broke out in 1914 had a serious impact on the political forces within India and their interaction with the British administration. While promising to support the war effort of the British rulers, Indian politicians sought from them in exchange reforms to allow better representation of Indians in the administration. In order to pursue this objective, they made efforts to bring together Hindu and Muslim representatives to speak unitedly—which led to the famous Lucknow Pact of 1916, where the Congress accepted the Muslim leaders' demand for separate electorates and came to an agreement with them over the distribution of seats in future representative bodies. But such compromises at the top could not eliminate the basic causes of Hindu-Muslim tensions at the ground level in Bengal, where they were often rooted in the age-old socio-economic conflict between the rich zamindars, moneylenders, or businessmen (who in most cases happened to be Hindus) and the poor tenants, peasants, artisans, or labourers (who were usually Muslims). Violent clashes between Hindus and Muslims continued to break out at frequent intervals during the second decade of the twentieth century, also, despite pacts between their leaders at the top.

As for militant nationalism, although the Bengal partition was revoked, armed revolutionaries were in no mood to give up their objective of overthrowing the colonial rule by force. In fact, their activities during this period spread beyond Bengal, the most daring demonstration being a bomb attack on Hardinge, the then British Governor-General in the new capital, Delhi, in December 1912. As the First World War broke out, revolutionary activities expanded beyond the shores of India. The Ghadr movement started in the USA. Indian émigré groups in Europe established contacts with fellow revolutionaries in India. Conspiracies were hatched to smuggle arms from abroad to launch an all out offensive against British rule. The colonial administration responded by violent suppression of all these attempts and under the draconian Defence of India Act of 1915, arrested thousands of young people and detained them for years without trial.

Above all, in rural Bengal, the poor continued to lead a life of poverty, exploited by landlords and moneylenders, and oppressed by the upper-caste gentry as in the past. Constructive village upliftment programmes to improve their lot, which Rabindranath expected the youth to engage in during the swadeshi movement, had not taken off. Increasing frustration with the slow pace of official reforms was driving the tenants and peasants in many parts of the country to organise movements to confront the zamindars with demands for radical changes in their socio-economic status.[18] It was these disquieting developments that loomed large in Rabindranath's mind when he started writing *Ghare Baire*, which came out in 1916. He found that on the political scene, Hindu-Muslim communal tensions remained as explosive as ten years ago. He also detected a resurgence of the same violent form of militant nationalism that had revolted him during his involvement with the swadeshi movement in 1905.

But more importantly, Rabindranath realised that things had not changed for the rural poor in the Bengal countryside since the 1905–07 days. It was this problem—the lot of the peasantry and their relationship with the zamindar—that occupied much of his thoughts in the decade following the days of the swadeshi movement.[19] It compelled him to introduce the poor tenant Panchu and other peasants in a narrative which otherwise would have remained predominantly a story of a triangular romance. In accordance with Rabindranath's perceptions about the agrarian scene and his notions about peasant-zamindar ties, Panchu and his comrades in *The Home and The World* end up either as victims of the oppressive zamindar-cum-moneylender Harish Kundu, or as supplicants at the doors of the benevolent and reformist zamindar Nikhilesh. The location of his story in the swadeshi period helped Rabindranath to revive and re-examine the concerns that were his preoccupations in his different roles as a zamindar, a disillusioned political observer, a proponent of socio-economic reforms, and a sensitive poet of human tragedy.

Notes

1. Quoted in the collection of Rabindranath Tagore's Bengali articles on rural society and economy called *Palliprakriti*, Vishvabharati, Calcutta, 1986, 269.
2. *Palliprakriti*, 268 . Ironically, here is a picture of a landlord desperately trying to pay back his creditors by collecting rents from his tenants who themselves were indebted to moneylenders. In fact, in the late nineteenth century—the time when Rabindranath visited his estates in East Bengal—and the early twentieth century, which is the backdrop of this novel, the peasantry were more burdened by debts that they owed to a new class of landlord-moneylender than oppressed by the rent collection of the old zamindars. According to contemporary records, the East Bengali cultivator's payments to his landlord in rent and other forms formed a small percentage,

while the burden of his debt to the moneylender during this period posed the biggest threat. Sugata Bose, *Peasant Labour and Colonial Capital: Rural Bengal Since 1770,* Cambridge University Press, 1993, Indian edition, 124–25.

3. Op.cit. *Palliprakriti*, 268
4. Ibid., 30.
5. Ibid., 30.
6. An analysis of the British colonial motives behind the 1905 partition and their political implications for Hindu-Muslim relations, in general, and zamindar-peasant relations, in particular, in Bengal is essential for an understanding of Rabindranath's presentation of the socio-economic complexities in Sukhsar, the estate owned by Nikhilesh. Curzon, on the eve of the partition of Bengal, in a speech in Dhaka, in February 1904, promised that the Bengali Muslims in the newly carved out province would recover the unity that they had enjoyed in the past when the Muslim nawabs had ruled Bengal. It was also propagated that the new province would provide more jobs for Muslims. Following this, soon after the partition of Bengal, in 1906, the Muslim upper- and middle-class politicians set up the Muslim League in Dhaka, claiming to safeguard and promote Muslim interests. It was soon to emerge as the major rival of the Hindu-dominated Indian National Congress. Amalesh Tripathi's *The Extremist Challenge* (Calcutta 1967) and Sumit Sarkar's *The Swadeshi Movement in Bengal 1903–8* (Delhi 1973) are important sources of information about the developments relating to the Bengali nationalist protest against the 1905 partition as well as the fissures in Hindu-Muslim relations that it led to. For an analysis of the political and economic implications of these developments for the rural poor in Bengal, see Tajul Islam Hashmi's *Ouponibeshik Bangla,* Papyrus, Calcutta, 1985, and Suprakash Ray's *Bharater Baiplabik Sangramer Itihash,* DNBA Brothers, Calcutta, 1980.
7. Cf. Sufia Ahmed, *Muslim Community of Bengal, 1884–1912*, OUP, Bangladesh, 1974.
8. Rabindranath's presidential address at the Provincial Conference in Pabna, *Falgun,* 1314 (Bengali calendar).
9. For a detailed account and a sensitive analysis of the Hindu-Muslim conflict in parts of East Bengal and the role of the Muslim mullahs and small landholders, Hindu zamindars and politicians, and the communication media of both the communities in the communal

riots, see Suranjan Das, *Communal Riots in Bengal 1905–1947,* OUP, Delhi, 1991, 38–58.

10. Cf. *Bengal District Gazeteers, Mymensingh.* Quoted in op.cit. Suprakash Ray 282–95.
11. Suranjan Das.
12. *Bengal District Gazeteers, Mymensingh.* Also see, Dr Bhupendranath Dutta, *Bharater Dwitiya Swadhinata Sangram,* Calcutta, 204–05.
13. *Sadupay* in *Rabindra-Rachanabali,* Kolkata, 1357 (Bengali era), 526.
14. Presidential address at the Provincial Conference in Pabna, *Falgun,* 1314 (Bengali era).
15. *Byadhi O Protikar,* Calcutta, 1907.
16. The image of the Rajput warrior was not a farfetched one for the Bengali readers of *Ghare Baire.* Generations of Bengali Hindu bhadraloks, from the last quarter of the nineteenth century till the early decades of the twentieth, were initiated into the concept of Indian nationalism by Bengali politicians and intellectuals who fed them with patriotic stories—some true, some fictitious—of heroism, chivalry, and self-sacrifice of the Hindu Rajput *ranas* in their battles against the Muslim Mughal emperors. Their courageous deeds were meant to serve as a model for the Bengali patriots in their fight against the British Empire. Tomes of Bengali literary pieces started pouring out during this period, extolling, romanticising, and mythologising Rajput valour. Their authors included stalwarts like Bankimchandra Chattopadhyay (in his novel *Rajshingha),* Romesh Chandra Dutta (in *Rajput Jeeban Sandhya*), Rangalal Bandyopadhyay (in his long narrative poem *Padmini Upakhyan*)—and later, even Rabindranath in a few of his poems in the collection titled, *Katha O Kahini.* Ironically, however, in order to valorise Rajput heroic exploits against the Mughals, these writers, had to depend for their information on a British historian who wrote a romanticised history of Rajasthan that was woven from facts and legends. This was James Tod's *Annals and Antiquities of Rajasthan.* Unfortunately, also, the demonisation of the Muslim Mughal rulers in these literary works, led in a large measure to the alienation of Muslims in Bengal from the pan-Aryan Hindu nationalist movement of that period.
17. Reports in contemporary Bengali newspapers quoted in Suranjan Das, 1991, 42.
18. Sumit Sarkar, *Modern India 1885–1947,* Macmillan India Limited, India, 1983, 156–07.

19. During the euphoria of the early days of the swadeshi movement, Rabindranath hoped that it would inspire young people to go to the villages and help the rural poor adopt modern agricultural practices and to reform their society in order to improve their lot. With this objective, in 1906, he sent his son, Rathindranath, son-in-law, Nagendranath Gangopadhyay, and a favourite pupil of his, Santosh Chandra Mazumdar, to the USA to learn scientific agricultural techniques. They came back by about 1910–11 and joined Rabindranath in village upliftment work in his estates. In fact, when Rabindranath was writing *Ghare Baire* in the 1915–16 period, he was himself engaged in such work. In the Kaligram *pargana* of his zamindari, consisting of a number of villages spread over several miles, he, with the help of a group of committed social workers, initiated a five-point programme to (i) provide the villagers with proper health and medical care; (ii) set up schools for free primary education; (iii) help them to dig wells, make roads, and clear forests; (iv) protect them from the professional moneylenders by giving them loans at reduced rates of interest; and, (v) induce them to settle their disputes through arbitration at the village level instead of resorting to the more expensive litigations (for an account of this experiment of Rabindranath's, see the various reports and letters quoted in *Palliprakriti*, op.cit. 250–62).

9

Understanding Panchu: Swadeshi, *Ghare Baire*, and the Lower-Caste Peasants of Eastern Bengal

SEKHAR BANDYOPADHYAY

I

At the time the Bengal partition scheme received official sanction on 4 July 1905, the province was submerged in an unprecedented political agitation that witnessed the contestation and negotiation between various forms of nationalisms. Rabindranath Tagore sought to write a critique of this contest into the narrative structure of his novel, *Ghare Baire*. At one end, he sought to situate that extreme form of nationalism which rested on an imagination of *desh* (country) as the supreme goddess, at whose altar extreme sacrifices were to be made; *Bande Mataram* (hail mother!) became the emotive slogan of this variety of exclusive and aggressive nationalism. At the other end, he indicated the existence of another broader strand of nationalism that did not want to confine itself to the worshipping of the abstract concept of motherland. Desh, in this construct, was not just the land, but consisted of its people. The goddess of this motherland did not supersede the supreme god who resided in the hearts of all human beings. This humanist nationalism was not exclusive and did not breed hatred, but was universalist in its epistemological focus and rested on the idea of improvement for all people.[1] However, both these forms of nationalism could succeed only if the masses were mobilised for their support. For this purpose, certain amount of coercion did not seem to be ill-advised to the devotees of the aggressive form as it had no programme that could immediately appeal to the rural poor. The other nationalism believed in social reforms, constructive programmes, and gentle persuasion as means of social mobilisation. Neither succeeded, not at least in the short run, and the swadeshi movement in Bengal, which incorporated both these trends, thus came almost to a dead end by 1908.

However, this weakening of the swadeshi was also the outcome of continuous contestation from other contending forms of nationalism of the poorer Muslim and lower-caste peasantry of eastern Bengal, which vehemently resisted the swadeshi leaders and volunteers with disastrous consequences for the movement. Tagore's rendition of the inner conflicts of swadeshi nationalism in *Ghare Baire* implies, towards the end, the existence of such resistance, but does not quite integrate that story into its narrative structure. In reality, to a very large extent, the mass mobilisation efforts of the swadeshi leaders failed, because coercion soon brought resistance and the constructive programmes were not sufficient enough to generate enthusiasm among the Muslim and Dalit[2] peasantry. Both communities now initiated their own counter-mobilisation campaigns in opposition to the swadeshi movement. And these campaigns emanated from a different historical consciousness and dissimilar ideological construction of the nation. Mobilisation of the Muslim peasants in eastern Bengal has already been discussed in detail by other historians.[3] Here we will muse over the responses of the

Dalit peasantry[4] represented in *Ghare Baire* by the pitiable character of Panchu, who suffered incessantly in the hands of the overzealous swadeshi volunteers and their overbearing zamindar patron, Harish Kundu.[5] We will try to show, however, that the Panchus of East Bengal did not only suffer in silence; they also spoke, resisted, and triumphed.

II

From the late nineteenth century, a new consciousness was becoming gradually visible among the Dalit population in Bengal, who were searching for their own identity within an emergent "nation-space"[6]. As marshy lands and forest tracts were being reclaimed in eastern and northern districts of the province, there was some relative improvement in the economic conditions of some of these marginal groups. Castes such as the Namasudras in the east and Rajbansis in the north emerged as settled peasant communities. The former consolidated their demographic presence with economic progress in the districts of Dacca, Faridpur, Bakarganj, Jessore, and Khulna, the latter doing the same in the northern districts of Rangpur, Dinajpur, and the adjacent areas of Jalpaiguri and Cooch Behar. A limited spread of education created a small critical leadership who became instrumental in mobilising these communities for claiming social status and demanding economic rights. Despite the relative social mobility enjoyed by these groups, this mobilisation became easier, as there was still a positive correlation between landholding and caste status in the East Bengal countryside. In other words, while these groups filled in the lower strata in the complex tenurial structure of rural Bengal, landholding was still monopolised by the traditional high-caste gentry belonging to the three castes of Brahmin, Kayastha, and Baidya, who continued to oppress and despise their low-caste tenants.

In 1872, the Namasudras, therefore, came together from across a large tract of four districts—Faridpur, Bakarganj, Jessore, and Khulna—to boycott the upper castes in protest against various forms of social disability. The movement continued for about six months and then declined gradually because of the poor peasants' inability to sustain the movement without any gainful employment. After the 1891 census, which sought to enumerate the castes, such efforts at mobilisation increased among all the Dalit groups. The Rajbansis had their first organisation launched in Rangpur in 1891, with the primary objective of registering their distinct caste status. The 1901 census, which aimed not only to enumerate these groups but also attempted to determine the ritual rank of each caste, led to further proliferation of such caste associations. By 1905, almost every Dalit group in Bengal had its own association, its own journal, whose sole objective was to mobilise their caste members around a new consciousness of self-respect and to have their reinvented respectable caste status recognised in the census returns, which, they believed, would provide legitimacy to such claims in the absence of any upper-caste sympathies for such social movements. Their attitude to British rule rested on a different reading of Indian history, where the establishment of the colonial state did not represent a break with the glorious past, as the nationalists constructed it, but as an improvement over a darker antiquity marked by casteism, untouchability, and the oppressive regimes of the Brahmins and the Rajas who upheld the rules of Manu.[7] By contrast, what British rule appeared to have offered them was a promise of equal citizenship within the structures of a modern state and, therefore, a possibility of reworking the familiar relations of power within their society. The issue of subjection to colonial rule—which was so important to leaders like Sandip and his followers in *Ghare Baire*—seemed too remote and abstract to them than their more immediate subordination to zamindari and Brahminical domination. There is no reason to believe that the Dalit in colonial India remained untouched or uninspired by modernity, although they derived different meanings out of it, appropriated only its selected aspects, and deployed them to ensure their own emancipation rather than the liberation of an abstract imagined motherland.[8]

To put it in another way, within the new public space of colonial India, the organised Dalit groups sponsored a different epistemology of political practice and promoted a new discursive field within which new rights were claimed, new debates were raised. The mainstream nationalist movement, under its high-caste bhadralok leadership, took little notice of let alone express any sympathy for such social developments. The Congress high command until 1917 failed to take any position on the issue of untouchability;[9] and the local Bengali nationalists had other priorities for their social and political agendas. Thus, when the swadeshi movement began, the lower castes of Bengal, barring a few individual exceptions, failed to identify with any of the dominant constructions of nationalism. Mobilising the lower-caste peasantry therefore became the most difficult challenge for the swadeshi leadership.

The Muslims in eastern Bengal, as is well known, saw the partition as a new beginning of their self-improvement within the realities of the cosmopolitan British Empire. What is less known, however, is the fact that Dalit groups such as the Namasudras also saw in the partition an opportunity to improve their condition and demanded the same political privileges as were being promised to the Muslims. Organisations such as the Dacca Namasudra Hitaishini Samiti or leaders of the Namasudra movement centred at village Orakandi in Faridpur district now got in touch with the Muslim leaders of the new province, declared that they were not part of the Hindu community, and prayed to the Lieutenant-Governor for the "same rights and privileges" that had been granted to the Muslims.[10] Within the context of the swadeshi movement, this political alliance between the Muslims and the Namasudras appeared to be a natural coalition of two underprivileged social groups equally despised and oppressed by the high-caste Hindu gentry.[11] And if the elite leaders of the movement saw in the partition an opportunity for self empowerment, the masses of Dalit peasants found it hard to identify with the swadeshi agenda as it had nothing to offer them. It was difficult for them to participate in the boycott campaign simply because indigenous goods were often more expensive than their imported alternatives. This reluctance soon appeared to be a major problem for the swadeshi leadership.

The swadeshi movement, soon after its beginning, was taken over by the educated bhadralok and zamindars, the two groups being socially connected to each other in many ways. As Rabindranath depicted vividly in *Ghare Baire*, the latter group with the help of their naibs now began to force their poor *raiyats* to observe swadeshi and applied various coercive measures to secure compliance. There is enough historical evidence to show that in the eastern districts of Bengal, such as Dacca, Faridpur, or Bakarganj, poor peasants were being subjected to intimidation and coercion when found buying foreign goods.[12] A particular brazen incident of coercion was reported from village Sholla in Dacca district where, before the puja festival in 1907, young volunteers went searching from door to door in the Namasudra peasant neighbourhood to see whether or not foreign goods had been bought on the occasion of the puja, and on one occasion even tried to strip a woman of the foreign cloth she was allegedly wearing. The volunteers came from mainly the well-to-do gentry families in the region and, therefore, although police action was taken and court proceedings were initiated, nothing really happened to them except minor jail sentences for two of the volunteers.[13] It was reported that such coercive practices had become widespread throughout East Bengal, where the zamindars were actively trying to prohibit the sale of foreign goods in their zamindaries "on pain of heavy fine or sound shoe-beating".[14] The excesses of Harish Kundu, the nationalist zamindar, described in *Ghare Baire,* were thus by no means just fictional imagination. Apart from these, the other indirect methods of coercion were to use the fear factor by systematically spreading rumours that cow and pig fat and bones were mixed with foreign salt and sugar, that all lands would soon be taken over by the government, new taxes would be imposed on various trees, and men in large numbers would be herded off to Assam to serve as indentured labour. Finally, women would be forced to remarry![15]

However, there were also other swadeshi leaders who realised that coercion would not lead to success for the movement. As nation meant the people, nationalism would not move forward if the masses were not mobilised. And this mobilisation could only take place through constructive social reforms, which would address the concerns for social justice and economic well-being of the lower-caste peasantry. In Faridpur, leaders, such as Ambika Charan Mazumdar, and the Faridpur District Association tried to mobilise the Namasudra peasantry in the district by taking up their grievances, particularly where it concerned the government, such as their being treated badly in jails.[16] Schools where Dalit children were educated were given funding on condition that the students would take the swadeshi vow.[17] In Bakarganj, Aswini Kumar Datta and the swadeshi Bandhab Samiti also sought to mobilise the Namasudras by patronising their education and by organising arbitration courts, which proposed to help the peasants out from the jaws of the expensive colonial justice system.[18] Both Mazumdar and Datta undertook extensive tours in their districts, addressing well-attended meetings and urging the peasants to boycott foreign goods. But the social programme they were offering was still insufficient to attract the attention of the Dalit peasants in rural East Bengal to the issue of swadeshi and boycott.

Such endeavours could not evoke any noticeable response, as both Mazumdar and Datta were substantial and authoritarian zamindars in their own regions, and most of their volunteers came from the same social classes, who could not easily relate to the grievances of the poorer lower-caste peasantry. Nor could the latter identify with the political programmes of the swadeshi movement, which they thought was "something that the babus ... [were] doing".[19] Therefore, by the summer of 1908, foreign sugar and salt were being openly sold in the Muslim and Namasudra villages of eastern Bengal, and where they faced opposition, they opened their own *haat* (rural market). In Jessore and Khulna, notices were circulated that those who would not use foreign goods would risk their houses being burnt down.[20] In some areas in these two districts the Namasudra and Muslim peasants joined forces against the local Brahmins and Kayasthas, leading to some serious incidences of breach of peace.[21] The violent riots that Tagore described towards the end of *Ghare Baire* were not just the expression of Muslim resistance to swadeshi; there was often participation by the lower-caste Hindu peasantry as well.

This situation alarmed the swadeshi leadership and the Bengali literati in general. Articles began to appear in the vernacular media, arguing that if Swadeshi did not make any sense to Dinu Mandal or Hamir Sheikh, it was bound to fail.[22] Meetings promising social privileges to Dalit peasantry were hastily convened in various parts of eastern Bengal. The Bengal Provincial Conference held in Pabna in February 1908 promised the Namasudras the services of the washermen, barbers, and bearers.[23] Two meetings were held in Faridpur in March, where Ambika Mazumdar assured the Namasudras that he would work for the improvement of their social status if they refrained from using foreign goods.[24] Such promises to offer the services of washermen and barbers were routinely repeated in other conferences as well, such as the Barisal District Conference held on 17–19 August 1908, which had a special session devoted to "improvement and reformation of society". In this conference, it was acknowledged repeatedly that the Namasudras were opposed to swadeshi because they were despised by all sections of Hindu society. If *swaraj* meant equal rights with Englishmen, how could these people be denied the privileges they were asking for? Hence, barbers and washermen were to be persuaded to serve these castes, and some of the zamindars present there even promised to ensure this in their respective zamindaries![25]

Such conferences, as expected, were, "reported … to have had little effect on the people more particularly addressed".[26] And the reasons are not difficult to find. Those who spoke at these conferences belonged overwhelmingly to the three upper castes of Bengal, the Brahmin, Kayastha, and Baidya; but no one ever uttered a word about accepting food and water from the hands of the Namasudras, which was one of the foremost demands of their caste movement since the 1870s. Instead, barbers and washermen shared all the flak for the degraded condition of the Dalit in Bengali Hindu society. Such evident lack of serious interest in social reform could hardly go unnoticed by an articulate community such as the Namasudras, who were fighting for the last two decades for social rights. Throughout the movement they hardly responded at all to such swadeshi overtures.

III

The Namasudra peasantry did not respond to the swadeshi movement also because of the counter-mobilisation efforts initiated by their own community leadership. Their caste movement had started in the late nineteenth century, and its major centre was village Orakandi in Faridpur district. By the beginning of the twentieth century it had mobilised the peasantry in a wide region of East Bengal, and its leaders such as Guruchand Thakur, who saw more advantage in the partition, now tried to convince their peasant followers that the swadeshi movement was primarily in the interests of the high-caste gentry, while they wanted to shift its burden onto the shoulders of the poor peasants. Such a caste-class conflation was not difficult to conceive of and popularise owing to the much too obvious composition of the swadeshi leadership and its immediate following, already mentioned above. Guruchand now began to argue that Namasudra peasants would derive more benefit out of a strategic alliance with the Muslims and through the patronage of the colonial government.[27] And in this counter-mobilisation, the Namasudra leadership was adequately supported by the Christian missionaries already active among such groups in the region. It was not unexpected that the new government of Eastern Bengal and Assam would provide enough incentive to divert their attention away from the nationalist propaganda.

Particularly close to the Namasudras was an Australian Baptist missionary, Rev C.S. Mead, who arrived at Orakandi in 1905 and by 1906 had established close contact with the Namasudra leadership and opened a mission in Orakandi, with various educational and philanthropic projects.[28] The date of his arrival and his choice of place for opening the mission are significant, although there is nothing to suggest a conspiracy theory. In 1907, the new government of Eastern Bengal and Assam announced its recruitment policy to be based on the proportional numerical strength of the communities. The policy was particularly targeted at the Muslims, but the depressed classes were also to be covered by it. And this raised expectations in the minds of the educated sections of such communities.[29] In this context, in the autumn of 1907, Rev Mead organised a Namasudra delegation, headed by Guruchand himself, to meet Sir Lancelot Hare, the Lieutenant-Governor of Eastern Bengal and Assam and himself secured an appointment. The delegation apprised Hare of the social conditions of the Namasudras, expressed their support for British rule and the partition, and appealed for more access to public education and employment. The meeting was followed by some high-profile public appointments from among the Namasudras and more generous government funding for educational institutions catering for Namasudra children.[30] This came as a sharp contrast to national schools, which were run by the samitis and which were being reported "defunct" because of the lack of adequate funding.[31]

It is not surprising, therefore, to find that the Dalit peasantry in East Bengal by 1908–09 had discovered their allies among the Muslims of East Bengal and in the administration of the new province of Eastern Bengal and Assam, and they felt increasingly alienated from the swadeshi movement and its high-caste gentry leadership. By early 1908, they were openly resisting the boycott movement by demanding "freedom of trade", and preferring to buy foreign goods even though sometimes they were costlier than their swadeshi substitutes. In some areas, they reverted to their old methods of resistance by taking recourse to social boycott of the upper castes, refusing them all kinds of services.[32] This articulate resistance was, however, also the result of deteriorating agrarian relations in East Bengal arising out of the commutation proceedings and embittering the relationship between the Namasudra tenants and their high-caste landlords.

As a result of a steep rise in the price of rice, the landlords in East Bengal since the 1870s were fast converting low cash-paying tenancies into produce rent-paying *barga* tenures, where the tenants were required to pay landlords a proportion, usually half but sometimes even two-thirds, of the produce. But in this system, the amount of produce could vary owing to the uncertainties of nature. To avoid this problem the landlords at the turn of the century sought to convert these tenures on one pretext or another into *dhankarari* tenures, where the tenants had to pay a fixed amount of paddy (so many *maunds*), regardless of the harvest. Thus when the harvest was bad and the prices were high, almost everything was taken away from the tenants, and when there was plenty and the prices low, they were left with the surplus production. But, when the Settlement operations started in the Bakarganj district in 1904, the peasants came to know that there was a provision under Section 40 of the Bengal Tenancy Act of 1885 that they could apply for commutation of their produce rents into cash rents. The landlords tried to frighten them off by suing large numbers of them for alleged arrears of pay, but this did not break their resolve. In 1908, the government "specially empowered" an Assistant Settlement Officer to deal quickly with the appeals for commutation, and within months he was flooded with applications. In most cases, high produce rents were replaced with easy cash rents, and this emboldened the peasants further. Under the leadership of some Christian converts, there was now an organised campaign to apply for commutation leading to armed confrontations in some areas between the Namasudra peasants and their high-caste landlords, many of whom were recognised leaders of the swadeshi movement.[33]

This conflict was not confined to Bakarganj alone, but was visible in Faridpur also, where disturbances between the Namasudra tenants and the high-caste landlords over dhankarari tenures were regular occurrences. In 1909, this agrarian tension erupted into various forms of violent actions on the part of the Namasudra tenants, ranging from petty housebreaking to haat looting. And, when the police intervened to maintain law and order, they also faced stiff resistance.[34] In 1909, in a vast region of Faridpur, Bakarganj, Mymensingh, and Jessore, the Namasudra peasants virtually declared a social boycott of the higher castes, refusing to accept food and water touched by them and denying them all social services. They also held meetings with the Muslims to plan joint resistance to the boycott movement forced on them by the swadeshi volunteers.[35] The political implications of these developments were not lost on the swadeshi leaders. In the last three months of 1909 and at the beginning of the next year, they organised a series of meetings at Namasudra-inhabited areas, where social privileges were promised in return for participation in the swadeshi movement. But, things did not move much, as, although the leaders made promises, the Hindu society was not yet prepared to change its familiar modes of social interaction.[36] Social tension in the East Bengal countryside and consequent rejection of the nationalist movement by the lower-caste peasantry therefore continued well into 1911.[37]

In 1911, there was an additional cause that further marred the relationship among the Hindu castes of Bengal. This was the census operation, which had become a popular vehicle for fulfilling the higher social aspirations of the lower castes throughout India. The census was looked at as a legitimate official apparatus which could "fix relative status of different castes and ... deal with the questions of social superiority." As already mentioned, this mentality was the result of the census of 1901, which had ventured to determine the social rank of every caste in India. And, now in 1911, the census office was flooded with applications for changes in caste nomenclature and ritual ranks, the sheer weight of these applications amounting to one and a half maund.[38] An important fallout of these census movements was the local hostility of the higher castes to such claimants of higher ritual status.[39] The divisive forces in Bengali Hindu society were unleashed to such a degree that an article in *Bengalee* had to come up with words of caution: "We have enough of unrest in these troubled times. Let nothing be done to add to its volume by riding rough-shod over the cherished caste sentiments of important groups of the Hindu community".[40]

As for the Namasudras of East Bengal, they organised an orchestrated campaign to send petitions to the Census Commissioner to have their new name, "Namasudra", officially recognised in the census reports and the hated previous appellation, "Chandal", completely dropped. The petition that went from Orakandi in Faridpur was recommended by Rev Mead.[41] Though not just because of this missionary patronage, their claim was finally accepted by the census authorities, and they were entered as Namasudras in the report of 1911. But, more important was the political consequence of this whole census campaign. The Bengal Census Superintendent, E.A.Gait, had announced in a circular in July 1910 that the "depressed classes" would be enumerated separately in the coming census. The nationalists at once saw in this circular a sinister political motive to reduce the numerical strength of the Hindu community vis-à-vis the Muslims, and this was particularly ominous, as the Dalit were already demanding separate political rights.[42] Indeed, the Morley-Minto Reforms of 1909, by granting the Muslims a separate electorate had stoked similar political aspirations among the politically articulate Dalit groups. Although the Gait Circular was withdrawn in December 1910, the Namasudras at the beginning of 1911 sent a petition to the government which claimed that "we have not the slightest connections with any of the Hindu communities... Thus we desire to be recognised by the Government as entirely a different community having separate claim to political privileges like Muhammadans."[43] This bold assertion of a separate identity and defiance of the epistemic domination of a hegemonic nationalism of the high-caste Hindu leadership of the swadeshi era were hardly the results only of government inducements, missionary encouragement, or Muslim conspiracy. This also indicated a catastrophic lacuna in the process of imagining our nation—a failure of the swadeshi nationalism to integrate the Dalit population by addressing their grievances and listening to their demands for social justice. No wonder that by 1911 the swadeshi movement was virtually over without securing Dalit support for its dominant nationalist political agendas.

IV

If we start from a non-essentialist position to regard nation as something not given, but a constructed or an "imagined community", then the swadeshi movement was undoubtedly an important moment in that process of imagining our nation. The experience of this construction of nation was fraught with contestation between varying and conflicting concepts of nation. Rabindranath's novel, *Ghare Baire,* admirably captured one aspect of that contestation. Concerned mainly with the conflicts of changing values within the nationalist Hindu bhadralok community, it focussed primarily on the contest between the two forms of middle-class perception of nationalism. One was exclusive and aggressive, manifestly derived from the modern Western concept of territorial nation that was supposed to find its fulfilment in the formation of an independent nation-state. But this idea of territory was imaginatively reconstituted into the notion of motherland by invoking the imagery of mother goddess from the cultural repertoire of Sakta Hinduism, which obviously did not appeal to the mostly Vaishnavite Dalit peasantry. The other nationalism, also derived from the Western discourse of modernity, went, however, beyond the narrow statist conception of nation. It was inclusive and universalist, based on the notion of constructive self-improvement for all, where the concept of nation was not constricted by the restrictive physical boundaries of the land, but incorporated an expansive concept of people. But neither appealed to the Dalit peasantry of eastern Bengal whose ideas of nationhood and citizenship emanated from their own day-to-day experience of economic oppression and social disability perpetrated on them by the same people who led the swadeshi movement.

The first group of proponents of swadeshi nationalism remained too insensitive to the grievances of Dalits and trivialised their pain. And, if Nikhilesh in *Ghare Baire* represented the second strand of constructive and humanistic nationalism, he was evidently a lonely warrior and his was a minority position. The social reforms that such protagonists of constructive nationalism proposed, their own orthodox Hindu society was not prepared to accept them. If Nikhilesh tried to invoke the glories of Guhak and Ekalabya, the low-caste heroes of the legends, the rest of his community, including his own wife, happily remained in their own comfort zones within the narrow circles of aristocracy, legitimated by the hierarchy of ritual order enjoined by Manu.[44] And, their economic constructive programmes were too infantile or insignificant to effect any real change in society or economy. Their patronising promises were often misconstrued and impenitently rejected; Chandranath Babu's attempts to teach Panchu the moral lessons of self-help could only manage to alienate him![45] The Dalit peasants in Bengal in the early twentieth century were not looking for patronage of the higher castes, but were trying to find their own voice, searching for their own identity, and looking for a place within the immanent public space of colonial India. They found very little in the swadeshi agenda that they could identify with.

On the other hand, it will be improper to suggest that the Dalit peasantry were loyalists or pro-British, as their support for the colonial state was conditional and not teleological. When the state supported their cause, as in the case of the commutation proceedings, they were all in favour of it. But, during the riots, when the police intervened to restore law and order and thus sought to protect the high-caste Hindu gentry, they faced equally stiff resistance. And, if the Dalit leadership saw in the partition or in the idea of separate electorate an opportunity for self-improvement, that ambition emanated from their long experience of deprivation and powerlessness. In their understanding of nationhood, the question of equal citizenship than the sovereignty of a rarefied and mystical motherland was more important. It would not be accurate to suggest that they were untouched by colonial modernity and lived in *puranic* times. On the contrary, they selectively appropriated aspects of that modernity to craft a different history of liberation of their own. It took a long time for the predominantly high-caste leaders of mainstream nationalism to understand or appreciate the significance of such discordant voices. But even then, these alternative imaginings of nationhood dwelled on the borders of "nation-space", as they remained outside the narrative map of Tagore's *Ghare Baire*, where Panchu, the "representative of all the poor peasants of Bengal", remained almost voiceless. He is a passive and placid character, weak and vulnerable—"emaciated in hunger, blind in ignorance".[46] He is only a recipient of one zamindar's wrath and another's patronage; he needs Chandranath Babu's adroit protection and moral training. His own understanding of nationhood remains untold in the narratives of bhadralok nationalism. However, we should also remember that a novel is not "history"—it has no obligation to provide a truthful narrative of the reality, although both the text and its author are located within that reality or in fact are products of that reality. So selective depiction and the silences become telling, as they situate the author within that reality and reveal the politics of the text.

Notes

1. See *Ghare Baire*, *Rabindra Rachanabali*, vol. 9, birth centenary edition, Calcutta, 1368 BS, 419, 424–25, 429, 466–67, 472–74, 477–78.

2. I am using here the word "Dalit" (oppressed) with great caution, knowing fully well that it was not in use in Bengal in the early twentieth century. However, I find this word more appropriate than to identify these groups as untouchables, as all of them were not regarded as untouchables in the strict sense of the term.
3. See for example, Sufia Ahmed, *Muslim Community in Bengal, 1884–1912,* Dacca, 1974; R. Ahmed, *The Bengal Muslims, 1871–1906: A Quest for Identity,* paperback edition, Delhi, 1996.
4. This essay is based on materials drawn from chapter 3 of my book *Caste, Protest and Identity in Colonial India: The Namasudras of Bengal 1872–1947,* Richmond, Surrey, 1997. Readers interested in more details on this subject may see this chapter titled: "Social Mobility and Politics in the Swadeshi Era, 1905–1911". Also for a broader discussion on the caste question in Bengal, see my *Caste, Politics and the Raj: Bengal 1872–1937,* Calcutta, 1990, and *Caste Culture and Hegemony: Social Dominance in Colonial Bengal,* New Delhi, 2004.
5. *Ghare Baire,* 479.
6. I have borrowed this expression from Homi Bhabha, "Introduction: narrating the nation", in H.K.Bhabha, ed, *Nation and Narration,* London and New York, 1990.
7. One may recall here Bimala's opening narrative in *Ghare Baire,* which represented how the elite households in Bengal, while absorbing some of the Mughal customs and desperately trying to domesticate colonial modernity were still governed by the rules of Manu and Parasar(408).
8. For more details on these movements, see my *Caste, Politics and the Raj,* chapters 3–4; *Caste, Culture and Hegemony,* chapter 1; and Swaraj Basu, *Dynamics of a Caste Movement: The Rajbansis of North Bengal, 1910–1947,* New Delhi, 2003.
9. On the Congress position on untouchability, see E. Zelliot, "Congress and the Untouchables, 1917–1950", in R. Sisson and S.Wolpert, eds, *Congress and Indian Nationalism,* Delhi, 1988.
10. Sitanath Biswas, *Jatitattva O Namasyakulodarpan,* (Theory of Caste and the History of Namasudra Lineage), Dacca, 1931, 157; Mahananda Haldar, *Sri Sri Guruchand Charit,* (biography of Guruchand), Calcutta, 1943, 403; Sufia Ahmed 257.
11. Raicharan Biswas, *Jatiya jagaran* (The Awakening of a Caste), Calcutta, 1921, 72–78.

12. "Summary of Position drawn up by Inspector General of Police, Bengal"; also private telegram from the Viceroy to the Secy. of State, GI, Home (Public), June 1906, Progs. Nos. 169–86, Notes, National Archives of India (hereafter NAI).
13. "Fortnightly Report on the Agitation in Eastern Bengal and Assam" (hereafter FR) for the second half of October 1907, GI, Home (Political), January 1908, Progs. No. 50; FR for the first half of November 1907, GI, Home (Political), January 1908, Progs. No. 52, NAI.
14. FR for the second half of November 1907, GI, Home (Political), January 1908, Progs. No. 53, NAI.
15. Confidential Diary of SP, Bakarganj, for the week ending 29 June 1907, GI, Home (Political), August 1907, Progs. No. 108, NAI; Confidential Diary of SP, Bakarganj, for the week ending 6 July 1907, GI, Home (Political), August 1907, Progs. No. 110, NAI.; "Weekly Report of the Director of Criminal Intelligence", (hereafter, WR), 8 January 1908, GI, Home (Political), B January 1908, Progs. No. 115, NAI.
16. Telegram, from the Magistrate, Faridpur to Chief Secy., GEB &A, 5 July 1907, GI, Home (Political), B July 1907, Progs. No. 197, NAI.
17. "Report on the National Schools in the Province of Eastern Bengal and Assam", Part I, GI, Home (Political), March 1909, Progs. Nos. 10–11, NAI.
18. Sarat Kumar Ray, *Mahatma Aswinikumar*, (Aswini Kumar the Great Soul), Calcutta, 1333 BS, 68–73, 97–98, 185, 261; Sureshchandra Gupta, *Aswini Kumar*, Barisal, 1335 BS, 206–07, 211, 357, 419, 552–53; Bipin Chandra Pal, "*Swargiya Aswini Kumar Datta*", (The Late Aswini Kumar Datta), *Bangabani*, vol.2 (2nd Half), No.6, *Magh* 1330 BS, 811–812; Surendranath Sen, *Aswini Kumar Datta*, Calcutta, nd., 33; "History of the Second Year of the Swadeshi Movement, 22nd Ṣraban, 1313–1314 BS.", "Supplementary Report on the Samitis in the Dacca Divn., Eastern Bengal and Assam", GI, Home (Political), Deposit, July 1909, No. 13, NAI.
19. Resumè of affairs in Bakarganj for 1907, GI, Home (Political), April 1908, Progs. No. 24, NAI.
20. Confidential Diary of SP, Bakarganj, for week ending 6 July 1907, GI, Home (Political), August 1907, Progs. No. 110, NAI.; Diary of Mr. Hughes-Buller, District Magistrate of Bakarganj, for the month of January 1908, GI, Home (Political), April 1908, Progs.

No. 24, NAI; WR, 11 April 1908, GI, Home (Political), 8 May 1908, Progs. No. 38, NAI.

21. G.S. Dutt, Magistrate of Khulna, to the Commissioner, Presidency Divn., 5 June 1911, GB, Political (Police), File No. P5R-1, B July 1911, Progs. Nos. 326–28, West Bengal State Archives, (hereafter WBSA).
22. Jogendranath Gupta, "*Prajasaktir Abhyuththan*", (The Rise of the Subject People), *Nabyabharat*, vol. 26, No.5, *Bhadra* 1315 BS, 275–276.
23. Resolutions of the Bengal Provincial Conference, (1908), Annexure-B, GI, Home (Political), March 1909, Progs. No. 10, NAI.
24. WR, 21 March 1908, Home (Political), GI, B April 1908, Progs. No. 48, NAI.
25. "Report of the Sadar Inspector of Police on the meeting of the 19th August held in the Raja Bahadur's Haveli", Appendix III, to the FR for the second half of August 1908, GI, Home (Political), October 1908, Progs. No. 104, NAI.
26. FR for the second half of August 1908, GI, Home (Political), October 1908, Progs. No. 104, NAI.
27. Mahananda Haldar, *Sri Sri Guruchand Charit*, (A biography of Guruchand), Calcutta, 1943, 168–76.
28. Ibid, 143–63, 176–84; C.S.Mead, *The Namasudras and Other Addresses* (Adelaid, 1911), 11, 14, 17, 22, 63, 116, 123.
29. Balaram Sarkar, *Namasudra Jnana Bhandar*, Faridpur, 1911, 14–22.
30. Naresh Chandra Das, *Namasudra Sampraday O Bangladesh*, Calcutta 1368 BS, 37–38; Mahananda Haldar, *Sri Sri Guruchand Charit*, 229–30.
31. "Report on the National Schools in the Province of Eastern Bengal and Assam (From 1 October 1908 to 30 June 1909)", GI, Home (Political), March 1911, Progs. No. 5, NAI.
32. Sumit Sarkar, *Swadeshi Movement in Bengal, 1903–1908*, New Delhi, 1977, 330–31.
33. See, *Final Report on the Survey and Settlement Operations in the Bakarganj District 1900 to 1908*, by J.C. Jack, Calcutta, 1915, 167–68 and Appendices under G.
34. FR for the latter half of January 1909, GI, Home (Political), March 1909, Progs. No. 105, NAI; WR, 9 October 1909, GI, Home (Political), B November 1909, Progs. No. 34, NAI; H. Le Mesurier,

Chief Secy, GEB&A, to Secy., GI, Home Department, 20 October 1909, GI, Home (Political), December 1909, Progs. No. 16, NAI.

35. Kaliparasanna Chakraborti, "*Bangalar Bartaman Hindu Samaj*", (The present day Hindu society of Bengal), *Nabyabharat*, Vol.27, No. 12, *Chaitra* 1316 BS, 642–3; "National Volunteers" in Eastern Bengal and Assam; Report on their Organisation, Extent and Numbers", GI, Home (Political), Deposit, August 1909, No. 26, NAI; WR, 7 August 1909, GI, Home (Political), B September 1909, Progs. No. 47, NAI.
36. "Report on the Political Situation in Eastern Bengal and Assam", [hereafter MR], for October and November 1909, GI, Home (Political), January 1910, Progs. No. 14, NAI; WR, 20 November 1909, GI, Home (Political), B January 1910, Progs. No. 49, NAI; 25 December 1909, GI, Home (Political), 8 February 1910, Progs. No. 127, NAI.
37. MR for February 1911, GI, Home (Political), April 1911, Progs. No. 20, NAI.
38. *Census of India* 1911, Vol. V, Part I, 440.
39. GI, Home (Political), April 1911, Prog. No. 20, NAI.
40. *Bengalee*, 2 October 1910.
41. Mahananda Haldar, *Sri Sri Guruchand Charit*, 255–58.
42. "Annual Report on Indian papers Published in the Bengal Presidency during the Year 1910", Calcutta, 1911, 36, GI, Home (Political) B July 1911, Prog. No.120, NAI.
43. MR for February 1911, GI, Home (Political), April 1911, Progs. No. 20, NAI.
44. *Ghare Baire*, 467.
45. Ibid., 477.
46. Ibid, 483, translation mine.

10

Mirjan from the Margins

Saswati Sengupta, Shampa Roy, Sharmila Purkayastha

Towards the end of the novel, *Ghare Baire*, on the personal front, in the world of ghare, order and poetic justice seem to be restored. Nikhilesh, his wife, and sister-in-law get ready to leave the rural estate for Calcutta. Sandip takes his bow revealing that he too perhaps has a conscience. But the tidy conclusion is splintered by events taking place baire, throwing into disarray what had appeared to be the imminent closure of the novel:

> Nikhil, the Muslim group is aroused. Harish Kundu's kutchery has been looted. That in itself does not arouse fear, but the way they have started outraging the women cannot be tolerated while there is life. (Chandranath Babu in Bimala's narrative, 206)[1]

The news of the marauding Muslim rioters draws from Nikhilesh the immediate response of action, "Then I will go." Nikhilesh races out on horseback, perhaps like the heroes of Bimala's childhood *rupkathas* (fairy tales) and perhaps also in keeping with his own residual notion of masculinity:

> We are men, freedom is our arduous endeavour: we will rush forward at the call of ideals, we have to rescue the captive Lakshmi by scaling the walls of the demon land..."(114).

And so the hero rushes out, but without his pistol, in keeping with his life of intellectual interiority. And so the novel ends, in *media res*, with the hero and all the ideals that he stood for, hovering uncertainly between life and death.

The subject of this article, however, is not Nikhilesh but the rioters who both disturb and draw the closure of the novel. These disruptive rioters are reported to be Muslims in the narrative even as in an earlier section they are represented as the oppressed peasantry of the Hindu landlords and gomastas.

> The History student remembered, "This I have seen with my own eyes, Gurucharan Bhadhuri, the Gomasta of the Kundus, had gone out to collect the revenue—a Muslim subject had nothing to buy or sell. He had only his young wife. Bhaduri said, you will have to pay with your wife. A candidate for the marriage was found, the money was paid. I am telling you, I could not sleep that night seeing the husband's tears. But however sad you feel, this I have learnt that when money has to be obtained then the man who can force the debtor to sell his wife is a better man than I—I can't do it, tears come to my eyes, that is why everything is washed out. If some one can save my country then they are these gomastas, these Kundus, these Chakrabartys" (135).

This confession by a young and educated Hindu student follower of Sandip's brand of swadeshi of the willing and cynical nexus which recognised oppression in the name of nationalism had stunned

Nikhilesh. It had drawn from him the resolve to protect his country from "these gomastas, these Kundus, these Chakrabartys." Yet, the conclusion appears to be a reversal of Nikhilesh's earlier promise. The discrepancy demands a reading of the novel outside of its central preoccupation with the upper-caste and upper-class Hindu protagonists and thus as also representing the plight of the Muslim peasantry and their redressal of wrongs in the fermenting context of the colonial government's separatist policy, an increasingly Hinduised swadeshi movement, and the growing political identity of the Muslim in the subcontinent. The popular reading of *Ghare Baire* is that of a story of the extramarital attraction of an upper-class, upper-caste Hindu wife of a devoted husband against the political backdrop of swadeshi. This reading disperses to the margins the narrative of consolidation of Muslim identity from being victims of physical coercion of rent collectors and the swadeshi brigands to becoming an organised body. Yet it can be recuperated:

> The news is this, the ryots of Kundu who bring their ware to the village mart have been subjugated. Nikhil's *amla* (clerks) secretly support us. They are putting pressure from within. The Marwaris are asking to be allowed to sell foreign cloth on the payment of a fine or else they will be ruined. The Muslims are refusing to be controlled (as narrated by Sandip, 117).
> Mirjan understood it all. He came directly to me and weeping with folded hands said, "*Huzoor*, I made a mistake now..." (Sandip,118).
> Those who go to court, we will set fire to their granary... (Sandip, 118).
> "The Maulvis have started coming from Dacca. They are inciting the local Muslims."
> (Nikhilesh in Bimala's narrative, 162).
> Soon after in one or two areas on the estate, where earlier the Muslims had as intense an antipathy to cow slaughter—such incidents are reported (Nikhilesh, 166).
> "I have received news, the Muslims have planned to seize me as a precious jewel and bury me in their graveyard" (Sandip in Bimala's narrative, 205).

On the one hand Sandip says that in the beginning of the andolan they "shouted themselves hoarse proclaiming that the Mussalmans are our brethren" but "have come to realize that we shall never be able to bring them wholly to our side. So they must be suppressed altogether and made to understand that we are the masters" (122). On the other hand, what the narrative recuperates is the growth of a Muslim identity in *Ghare Baire,* from being victims of rapacious landlords, having to submit to the demoniac will of the swadeshi brigade, to the aggressive rejoinder in rioting at the Kundu estate. Nikhilesh may believe that "Mussalmans are a necessary part of United India", and the prominent Hindu tenants of Nikhilesh may concede that there was no "visible symptom of the disease" earlier, but the belief is proved inadequate in the world of the novel on two counts: the obvious anti-Muslim feelings within the swadeshi movement and the corresponding articulation by the Muslims for a separate identity symbolised, for instance, through the reference to cow-slaughter (123, 166).

Historical facts testify that in the initial stages of the partition of Bengal (about 1903), Muslims were as opposed to the question of division as were the Hindus, and many prominent leaders denounced it. Nawab Salimulah Khwaza Atiqullah (1876–1945), Abdur Rasul (1872–1917), Abdul Halim Ghaznavi (1879–1956), the peasant leader Ismail Hossain Shiraji (1880–1931), are some of the eminent Muslim leaders who protested against the partition of Bengal and cautioned against the stirring of communal feelings. However, Bengali solidarity across religious lines was shaky from at least the last quarter of the nineteenth century and instances of communal tensions were noted from the 1880s onwards over issues such as cow protection, anti-Muslim content of Hindu *jatra* theatres (which were open-air performances), religious processions, or land disputes between Hindu landlords and Muslim tenants. The Titagarh (1896) or the Talla (1897) riots showed the fragile nature of suburban life where slight provocations could and did result in major riots.[2] The socio-economic context of deteriorating relations between the two communities was located largely in land relations. Census records of 1881 showed that more than 90 per cent of the Muslims belonged to the agricultural section, and barring a handful who were "non cultivating land owners", the vast majority were tillers of the soil.[3] Thus, the stratifications in the agrarian structures are often said to coincide largely with the Hindu-Muslim communal division in eastern and northern Bengal (while in western and south-western Bengal this divide corresponded roughly, if not spectacularly, with the distinction between the predominantly upper-caste bhadralok elite and the middle-caste cultivating peasants). "In cultural terms 'landlordism' in this region was generally perceived as something practised principally by upper-caste Hindu landlords. To this was added in the predominantly jute-growing districts of northern Bengal the presence of the *paschima* (usually Marwari) moneylender."[4] This social and economic base of unequal relations between the two communities played a big role in exacerbating communal tensions, and during the swadeshi movement, the Hindu landlord was perceived as particularly oppressive and coercive. The economic differences were also often aggravated by the caste Hindu social practice of dividing humanity along a purity-pollutant axis.

One of the disturbing features about communal tensions in this period is the manner in which the Hindu communalists manufactured and reproduced the issue of cow-slaughter within popular psyche. Ritual slaughter (*korbani)* was an annual event, but most poor Muslims could hardly afford it and even beef eating was not a regular activity amongst the average Muslims. But, wider militant Hindu campaigns such as Dayananda's *Gaurakshini sabha* (1882) or local ones initiated by the Hindu Bengalis and Marwaris in the 1890s made the issue of cow-slaughter into a hysterical one, and the British administration's efforts at preventing communal tensions only backfired as the fine print of official rules, such as definition of "public roads" or religious processions, were fiercely contested. The Muslim reaction to the Hindu agitation was equally fierce as the various *anjumans* (religious assemblies) and official bodies such as the CNMA (Central National Muhammadan Association) urged the average Muslim to resist all Hindu coercive efforts ranging from the economic to the political and the social. Thus, communal tensions could and did erupt over apparently very flimsy and unconnected issues and charged popular sentiments on either side were ever ready to boil over.

Besides land relations and cow-slaughter, the Hindus and Muslims had other reasons for parting ways. The 1871 census and the subsequent one, a decade later, produced some startling facts about the Muslim community, namely, that they comprised nearly half the population (48 per cent), that most were located in poor marshy areas of eastern Bengal, and that the majority did not have the same advantages in terms of colonial education and jobs as the upper-caste Hindus (the bhadraloks) did.[5] Sekhar Bandyopadhyay in his discussion of the "evolution of the politicized communitarian identity in the late nineteenth century" talks of the political role played by the census as "it made religion its fundamental ethnographic category for classifying demographic and developmental data. Each census report sought to give concrete and recognisable shape to the religious communities by discussing the numerical size of such groups, their percentage to the whole population indicating their majority or minority status in each region and in the country as a whole. The result of this census taxonomy was the new concept of "religion as a community". Religion no longer meant just a set of ideas, but came to be identified with "an aggregate of individuals united by formal official definition", sharing supposedly the same characteristics and conscious of their comparative demographic as well as socio-economic position vis-à-vis other communities."[6] This tended to marginalise the other revelation of the colonial census that the entire Muslim community was internally fragmented along lines of ethnicity, caste, class, and social power The separation between the *ashraf* (high) and *atrap* (low) was both racial and economic, and the absence of an intermediary group added to the existing internal divisions—so much so that the average Muslim peasant had much more in common with his Hindu brethren as they spoke the same language, were divided into similar *jatis* like the Hindus, shared a common rural life, and even participated in similar rituals and festivals.[7]

Through the nineteenth century, the various revivalist movements such as the Wahabis, Faraizis, or the Tariquahs concentrated on giving a common religious character and cohesion to an otherwise splintered and divided community. For the poor peasant, who mainly depended on the local and, often, illiterate *maulvi* and *pirs* for religious education, the revivalist movements brought about significant changes. The awareness of religious identity, importance of doctrinal tenets, or the significance of Urdu over Bengali forced interaction within the community, which helped in mobilising the rural Muslim masses.[8] The recognition of lack of proper education and job prospects created amongst the educated and urban Muslims the need for political organisations that could bargain for better advantages from the English. Educated and sophisticated leaders such as Syed Ameer Ali or Nawab Abdul Latif founded not communal but exclusivist Muslim organisations whose motto was "being Muslims for Muslims".[9] Thus, while the divide between the elite and the rural masses remained a serious one, the importance of doctrinal Islam over popular religion, the question of "Muslim backwardness" in terms of colonial education and jobs, and the need to assert a non-Bengali political identity shaped the emerging Muslim identity through the latter half of the nineteenth century.

In the early months of the swadeshi campaign, there was Hindu-Muslim solidarity, but soon after there was a dissociation and a growing perception that the ideas of Hindu extremism were against Islam. Further, Lord Curzon's determined efforts to sell partition and create an exclusive Muslim political community in the new province also bore fruit. In his speech in Dhaka (in 1904), "he assured the Muslims that the plan envisaged the creation of a centre of Muslim power in Dacca 'which would invest the Mahommedans in Eastern Bengal with a unity which they have not enjoyed since the days of the old Mussalman viceroys and kings.'"[10] Moreover, the call of boycott of foreign goods alarmed the Muslims, as they feared that the socio-economic domination of the Hindu traders and landlords would exploit the poorer Muslims even more. It was argued that the Hindu landlord was determined to force swadeshi ideas on his Muslim tenants and to join the anti-partition movement. And the particularly Hindu moves adopted by the movement, such as "*Bande Mataram*" as the national slogan, or the introduction of the cult of Shivaji as the national hero, or the induction of Hindu goddesses for inspiration alienated the

Muslims even more. The formation of the Mohammaden Provincial Union in 1906 and the All India Muslim League in Dhaka in the same year sealed the formation of separatist politics, and the very first resolution made by the League was to welcome the partition as it was seen as beneficial for the Muslim community. The Comilla riots in March 1907, the riots in Jamalpur in April, and the Mymensingh riots of 1907 underlined the extreme communal tensions between the two communities.

The annulment of partition in 1911 was a setback for the Muslims, but the Bengali Hindus also were not overjoyed as the importance of Calcutta had diminished and the entire swadeshi agitation had also run out of steam. However, the importance of the partition in 1905 was enormous: it became the forerunner of the larger and later Indian freedom struggle, it produced the beginnings of separatist politics, and it opened the gulf between Hindus and Muslims as never before.

In the fictional world of *Ghare Baire*, Nikhilesh's Muslim peasants had disliked the practice of cow-slaughter as much as their Hindu neighbours, though with the growth of swadeshi activities in the area, including the preparation of Durga puja by Harish Kundu and Sandip for which the tenants would be coerced to pay, one or two instances of cow-slaughter are reported. Nikhilesh's reasoned argument over the specious nature of religious symbolism that glorifies the cow but sacrifices the buffalo in the autumnal ritual worship of the Hindu mother goddess cannot stem the fanaticism of religious beliefs any more than the fact that the news of cow-slaughter on his estate is brought by a Muslim peasant, who also registers his protest (166). Nikhilesh recognises a "stubborn will" to be at work in this display of religious identity and that, "Today it is possible to use the Muslim as a weapon against us, because we have made it so..." (17). The steady growth of a collective political will among the Muslims is actually a significant strand of the novel's critique of the swadeshi as a separatist political movement whose final culmination was the partition of the subcontinent in 1947. The fascist nature of Hindu nationalism is evident from the manner in which Sandip and Harish Kundu decide that all the tenants must pay for the Hindu ritual worship of Mahisasuramardini, the militant mother goddess, or the brutal manner in which Mirjan's livelihood is destroyed by Sandip and his followers in a bid to enforce boycott of foreign goods. Mirjan acquiesces, but Sandip forgets to pay him the hush money (Rs 2000) or bribe the police (as they had traced the man who had sunk Mirjan's boat); the arrogant Hindu leader can dispense with the poor Muslim easily. The brilliance of the plot lies in its effortless depiction of how political opportunity rides shamelessly on the back of poverty and exploitation. Mirjan and Panchu are almost interchangeable, despite their disparate economic conditions, in their story of woes and distress, as the upper-class and upper-caste leaders and followers exploit both. But, there is one significant difference: Mirjan is pragmatic enough to acquiesce. Perhaps he knows that there will be no saviour for him unlike Panchu who remains belligerent and phlegmatic.

With brash arrogance Sandip asserts that the suppression of the Muslims is necessary for future gains of a Hindu state, and he constructs a past of the oppressed Hindu Bengali and the Muslim invader to legitimise such coercion: "These two goddesses represent the two images the Shakti of the country from whom the Bengali asked for the boon of vanquishing the foe during the Muslim rule"(127). Yet, the same Sandip also admits cynically that, "This is hypnotism…without which the lowly cannot survive" (125). The hypnotic value of Sandip's statement lies in its simplistic construction of a history in which Muslims were foreign invaders and foes of the Hindus, who were, by implication, therefore the truly indigenous population of India. In their search for a "viable cultural foundation for nationhood", cultural nationalists like Sandip, frequently and deliberately resorted to this fallacious construction of the medieval past in order to arouse passions against an alien rule and to construct a unified and combative Hindu identity.[11] Sandip, the articulate and educated Hindu leader, seeks to consolidate and justify his claims of nationhood by insisting on the existence of an intrinsic and metaphysical essence through Indian history which only needed to be retrieved for the revivification of the Indians and for the legitimation of their current political activity. This metaphysical essence is manifested as the Hindu religious tradition supposedly rooted in classical Sanskrit texts, which was meant to give the Hindus a sense of a unified identity in opposition to an alien rule. Thus Hinduism, which was "not a uniform monolithic religion but a juxtaposition of flexible religious sects", was evoked as a monolith located in a high *shastric* tradition.[12] This reconstituted Hinduism, which marginalised the more liberal and fluid folk traditions, "largely reflected the Brahminical view of the high-caste reformers."[13] Needless to say, it ended up alienating the Muslims, the non-Brahmins, and the untouchables. It is pertinent to note that Sandip, who believes that "they must be absolutely suppressed", provocatively decides to organise the ritual worship of the goddess Mahisasuramardini, symbolising Hindu militancy, at the fair of Hussein Gaji on Nikhilesh's estate where "lakhs of people congregate" (124, 131).

The framework of Indian history as mobilised by men like Sandip was the one that had been already put in place by old colonial thinkers, both by Orientalists like William Jones and Anglicists like James Mill. William Jones and other Orientalist scholars like him, keen to find the "pure" form of Hindu law and the "real" tradition of the Hindus—which they were quite sure resided in old texts rather than in the actual lived practices of the people—privileged the shastric tradition and consequently projected the Aryan society that apparently produced these texts as representing a so-called Golden Age in the history of India. The necessary corollary to such glorification of the Aryan civilisation as the true depository of a normative form of Hinduism was also the construction of subsequent ages, especially the medieval period as the time of decline and degeneration of this true Indian/Hindu culture. James Mill's seminal work, *A History of British India* (1840), while rubbishing the Golden Age theory, continued the division of Indian history into three distinct eras: Hindu, Muslim, and British and the fallacious categorisation of the previous periods as based on the religious affiliation of the dynasties.[14] The power of this kind of historiography becomes visible amongst nationalist writers when a great deal of exhortatory, patriotic writings composed in the post-Mutiny period borrowed these frameworks of history and celebrated the effective defeat or supercilious forgiveness of the "Muslim" foe by "Hindu" rulers. In Bhudev Mukhopadhyay's account of the battle between Ahmad Shah Abdali and the Maratha forces written in 1876, for instance, the Maratha commander declares that although the Muslims had always mistreated the Hindus, the Hindus were prepared to forgive them. In a grand council of the kings of India, a distinction is thus made between India's "natural" and "adopted" children:

> Although India is the true motherland of only those who belong to the Hindu *jati* and although only they have been born from her womb, the muslims are not unrelated to her any longer. She has held them at her breast and reared them. The Muslims are therefore her adopted children.[15]

Given that this kind of historical understanding was the basis of the political mobilisation of the nationalist leaders like Sandip, it was hardly surprising that they failed to get the sympathy or support of the Muslims. However, since the nationalists saw the principal conflict as being with the imperial government, it seemed not to matter to them that their strategies based on simple binaries and fixed stereotypes had become irretrievably intertwined with bigotry, prejudice, and sectarianism.

These simple binaries and fixed stereotypes and the bigotry they invariably give rise to, is precisely what the novel *Ghare Baire* critiques by mapping a more complicated terrain of social relations and lived practice. The existence of Nikhilesh's family as a Hindu zamindar since the Mughal-Pathan days, the presence in Nikhilesh's Calcutta college of a Muslim friend from Lucknow who had got him a pair of shoes for Bimala (88), Kasem who had guarded Nikhilesh's revenue for twenty-five years (169), the Muslim peasant who protests against cow-slaughter (166), demand a more complex reading of history as a narrative of cross-religious alliances as well as collusion of class and caste oppressions than Sandip is willing to formulate. One gets to know from Bimala's narrative that:

> The customs of my conjugal family are tied to ancient practice.

> Some of its manner and rules are of the Mughal-Pathan's, some of its prescription of Manu-Parashar's. But my husband is totally modern. (6)

The world that Bimala—and Nikhil—inhabit is thus a composite world, a compositeness that is registered in the Bengali original with the Persian words *kayda-kanun* inhabiting the same sentence as the Sanskrit word *vidhan* signalling Bengal's plural heritage. Brahminical and Islamic culture have thus shaped Nikhilesh's family, helped locate him in an elite relation to his society, allowing an access to the "modern" (read English) influence later on. Nikhilesh's most prominent heritage of the Mughal-Pathan is his privileged means of livelihood—the zamindari.

In the agrarian society of Bengal, the zamindars were the dominant socio-economic group. The term coined around AD 1400 from the Persian words *zamin* (land) and *dar* (holder) in the Mughal administrative system referred to the intermediate social group between the state and the mass of peasants, who held vast tracts of land on a hereditary basis subject to the payment of stipulated amounts to the Nawab Subedar of Bengal. Murshid Quli Khan, appointed as the *Dewan* (revenue minister) in 1700 by Aurangzeb, restructured the zamindari system in the province, which survived through the nawabi period. He is attributed with the creation of a new landed aristocracy in Bengal, and the most powerful Hindu zamindars of mid- and late-eighteenth century Bengal acquired the bulk of their estates under him. On August 1765, the Mughal emperor bestowed upon the Company the office of Dewan and the right to collect the territorial and custom revenues of Bengal, Bihar, and Orissa. The actual collection of revenues continued to be farmed out to zamindars.[16]

Gesturing as it does towards this nuanced reading of the complex history of Bengal, the novel clearly indicates that Muslim separatism was not the pre-ordained or invariable consequence of primordial differences between Hindus and Muslim. Rather it had resulted from the deliberate and strategic manipulation of the divisive symbols of religious identity by the elite groups of both communities in economic and political competition with each other. When at the end of the novel, Sandip drives off into the sunset after a surprising and brief display of conscience, it is the thorns that he had helped sow that burn the village and destroy the possibility of its syncretic identity. The novel is deeply critical of the manner in which elite leaders like him appropriated the right to define the identity of the nation, even as they called it the "nation's awakening to self-consciousness" and masked their own political ambitions and interests with the rhetoric of group mobilisation.[17] The dream of "freedom" held out by cultural nationalists like Sandip is thus revealed as being hollow and false, since its programme for promoting solidarity against the imperial power also unabashedly allowed differentiation from and coercion of the Muslims as well as the lower-caste peasantry.

Despite this critique, however, the rioters at the end of the novel are referred to as being nameless and faceless Muslims. In fact, communal tensions in the area are shown to be a result of the inflammatory speeches made by the mullahs from Dhaka, who are sent to counter the Hindu boycott agitation. The last event in the novel, the communal riot, is shown to be a consequence of Mussalmans going out of hand and dishonouring the Hindu women in the Kundu estate. The tragic irony is that Nikhilesh himself, for all his liberal beliefs and efforts, becomes a victim of "Muslim initiated riots". Why then, after having undermined with such deftness the kind of destructive communal stereotypes that vitiate relations between Hindus and Muslims, does the novel end by consolidating the stereotype of the violent and sexually uncontrolled Muslim mob? Since, the blame for the final catastrophe is made to fall almost entirely on the nameless and faceless Muslim rioters and not on the Hindu communalists, is one to conclude then that Tagore's genius balked at the idea of crucifying the majoritarian agenda however convincing and historically justifiable, and instead decided to play the "fair game" of showing an even-handed nature of justice and fair play? The change in the tenor of the novel's attitude to the communal issue is indeed vexing.

The key to a different understanding of the last riot might, however, lie in paying keener attention to the significant fact that the rioters attack the mansion of Harish Kundu, not Nikhilesh. A closer inspection of this distinction points to the possibility of social imperatives other than communal friction at work behind this outbreak of violence. Given the fact that Harish Kundu has been quite clearly represented in the text as a terrifyingly cruel landlord, does the violent targeting of his mansion by the rioters, in fact, signal the collective anger of the oppressed peasants against this agent of social and economic oppression rather than religious animosity? Since the incident is reported as a Hindu-Muslim riot at a time when communal passions run high and the focus of the novel subsequently shifts to Nikhilesh's act of selfless courage and Bimala's contrition, the possibility of looking at the attack as having other dimensions, remains unexplored in the text. The retrieving of this alternative reading of the concluding section based on attention to neglected evidence drawn from within the text, is not prompted by any desperate urge to affirm Tagore's liberal credentials. Rather, it is prompted by the urge to look at the question of identity formation and communal conflict in terms of prevalent socio-economic contexts and not through the limited explanatory frames provided by contemporary cultural nationalists.

Notes

1. Rabindranath Tagore, *Ghare Baire,* 1916, Kolkata, Viswabharati, 1994, 22. All future quotations refer to this edition of the text.
2. For a detailed understanding of communalism in this period, see Suranjan Das, *Communal Riots in Bengal (1905–1947),* New Delhi, OUP, 1991.
3. Rafiuddin Ahmed, *The Bengal Muslims: 1870–1906, A Quest for identity,* Oxford, 1981, 2.
4. Partha Chatterji, *Bengal 1920–1947. Volume I. The Land Question,* Calcutta, K. P Bagchi, 1984, 129.
5. See Sekhar Bandyopadhyay, *From Plassey to Partition: A History of Modern India,* Delhi, Orient Longman, 2004, 263.
6. Bandyopadhyay, 263.
7. See Rafiuddin Ahmed's *The Bengal Muslims: 1870–1906, A Quest for identity,* Oxford, 1981, for a thorough discussion on the same issue.
8. Pradip Kumar Datta also talks of an enormous expansion in Muslim-controlled newspapers as having taken place from the days of the swadeshi. In the rural areas, almost from the end of the nineteenth

century, there was the production and proliferation of Improvement tracts directed at rural Muslims, which defined their identity in communal terms by stressing everyday practical activities and providing pragmatic and organisational suggestions, which would help strengthen their community ties. These tracts, also written in the manner of the *punthis,* which were traditionally the reading material of the rural Muslims in the leisure hours, would therefore have had the kind of immediate appeal that contemporary writings on community-based reservation of seats in educational institutions and government employment could have had. See Pradip Kumar Datta, *Carving Blocs: Communal Ideology in Early Twentieth Century Bengal*, New Delhi, OUP, 1999, 65–68.

9. Ahmed, 163.
10. See Ghosh and Mukhopadhyay, 25.
11. Partha Chatterji, *Nationalist Thought and the Colonial World: A Derivative Discourse?,* London, Zed Books, 1986, 75.
12. Romila Thapar, "Syndicated Moksha?", *Seminar*, no. 313, 1985, 22.
13. Christophe Jaffrelot, *The Hindu Nationalist Movement and Indian Politics 1925 to the 1990s,* London, Hurst and Company, 1996, 13.
14. Mill does not call the third era "Christian", because for him the British rule was essentially secular, neutral, and based on the rule of equalising law.
15. See Partha Chaterjee 111. Chatterjee goes on to then talk about other writings that talked of history and imagined nationhood in alternative ways such as Akshaykumar Maitreya's *Sirajudaullah* (1898). However, these he says, "became submerged in the last hundred years by the tidal wave of historical memory about an Arya-Hindu-Bharatvarsha".
16. Ranajit Guha, *A Rule of Property for Bengal: An Essay on the Idea of Permanent Settlement,* Paris, Mouton & Co., 1963. John R. McLane, *Land and Land Kingship in 18th Century Bengal,* Cambridge, Cambridge Univ. Press, 1991. H.V. Bowen, *Revenue and Reform: The Indian Problem in British Politics,* (1757–1773), Cambridge, Cambridge Univ. Press, 1991. Chitta Panda, *The Decline of the Bengal Zamindars: Midnapore 1870–1920,* New Delhi, OUP, 1996.
17. "Nationalism is not the awakening of nations to self-consciousness: it invents nations where they do not exist." See Ernest Gellner, "Nationalism" in *Thought and Change,* London, Weidenfield and Nicholson, 1964, 169.

Select Bibliography

Primary Works

1. Tagore, Rabindranath. 1903. *Chokher Bali, A Grain of Sand.* 2003. Translated by Sreejata Guha. New Delhi: Penguin Books .
2. Tagore, Rabindranath. 1908. *Gora.* Translated by Surendranath Tagore. 1980, reprint. Madras: Macmillan.
3. Tagore, Rabindranath. 2000. *Selected Short Stories.* Edited by Sukanta Chaudhuri. *The Oxford Tagore Translations.* New Delhi: OUP.
4. Tagore, Rabindranath. 1916. *Ghare Baire The Home and The World.* Translated by Surendranath Tagore. Macmillan, 1919; Penguin India, 1999.
5. Tagore, Rabindranath. 2004. *The Home and The World* translated by Nivedita Sen. New Delhi: Srishti Publishers.

Secondary Works[1]

1. Ahmed, Rafiuddin. 1981. *The Bengal Muslims, 1871–1906: A Quest for Identity.* New Delhi: OUP.
2. Ahmed, Sufia. 1974. *The Muslim Community of Bengal, 1884–1912.* Dhaka: OUP.
3. Bandyopadhyay, Sekhar. 1990. *Caste Politics and the Raj: Bengal 1872–1937.* Calcutta.
4. ——. 2004. *Caste, Culture and Hegemony: Social Dominance in Colonial Bengal.* New Delhi: Sage Publishers.

1. This is a selected list of critical works on Tagore relevant to an understanding of the period, published in English or translated from Bengali into English. An exhaustive body of criticism on Tagore's writings as well as on the historical context is of course available in Bengali.

5. ——. 2004. *From Plassey to Partition: A History of Modern India.* Delhi: Orient Longman.
6. Bhattacharya, Tithi. 2005. *The Sentinels of Culture: Class, Education and the Colonial Intellectual in Bengal, 1845–1885.* New Delhi: OUP.
7. Burstyn, Joan N. 1980. *Victorian Education and the Ideal of Womanhood.* London: Croom Helm.
8. Carpenter, J. E. 1979. *The Life and Work of Mary Carpenter.* London: Macmillan.
9. Chakrabarti, Hiren. 1992. *Political Protest in Bengal: Boycott and Terrorism, 1905–1918.* Calcutta: Papyrus.
10. Chatterji, Partha. 1984. *Bengal 1920–47: The Land Question.* Calcutta: K.P. Bagchi.
11. Chatterji, Partha. 1986. *Nationalist Thought and the Colonial World: A Derivative Discourse?* London: Zed Books.
12. Das, Suranjan. 1991. *Communal Riots in Bengal, 1905–1947.* New Delhi: OUP.
13. Datta, P. K., ed. 2003. Rabindranath Tagore's *The Home and the World: A Critical Companion,* Delhi: Permanent Black.
14. Datta, P. K. 1999. *Carving Blocs: Communal Ideology in Early Twentieth Century Bengal.* New Delhi: OUP.
15. Forbes, Geraldine. 1996. *Women in Modern India.* Cambridge: Cambridge Univ. Press.
16. Ghose, Nityapriya and Ashoke Kumar Mukhopadhyay, eds. 2005. *Partition of Bengal: Significant Signposts, 1905–1911.* Kolkata: Sahitya Samsad.
17. Guha, Ranajit. 1963. *A Rule of Property for Bengal: An Essay on the Idea of Permanent Settlement.* Paris: Mouton and Co.
18. Guha-Thakurta, Tapati. 1992. *The Making of a New 'Indian' Art: Artists, Aesthetics and Nationalism in Bengal, c. 1850–1920.* Cambridge: OUP.
19. Murshid, Ghulam. 1983. *Reluctant Debutante: The Response of Bengali Women to Modernisation, 1849–1905.* Rajshahi: Rajshahi Univ. Press.
20. Ray, Niharranjan. 1967. *An Artist in Life: A Commentary on the Life and Works of Rabindranath Tagore.* Trivandrum: Univ. of Kerala Press.
21. Ray, Rajat Kanta. 1994. *Social Conflict and Political Unrest in Bengal, 1875–1927.* Delhi: OUP.

22. Sangari, Kumkum and Sudesh Vaid, eds. 1989. *Recasting Women: Essays in Colonial History.* New Delhi: Kali for Women.
23. Sarkar, Sumit. 2002. *Beyond Nationalist Frames: Relocating Postmodernism, Hindutva, History.* Delhi: Permanent Black.
24. ——. 1983. *Modern India, 1885–1947.* New Delhi: Macmillan India Ltd.
25. ——. 1973. *Swadeshi Movement in Bengal, 1903–1908.* New Delhi: People's Publishing House.
26. Sarkar, Tanika. 2001. *Hindu Wife, Hindu Nation.* New Delhi: Permanent Black.
27. ——. 1999. *Words to Win, The Making of Amar Jiban: A Modern Autobiography.* New Delhi: Kali.
28. Tripathi, Amalesh. 1967. *The Extremist Challenge: India between 1890–1910.* Bombay: Orient Longman.

Index